Faith-Filled Catholic Women's Bible Study Program

for use with the

Faith-Filled Catholic Women's Bible

and the

Faith-Filled Catholic Women's Bible Music CD

22 Session Plans for Catholic Women

Fireside Catholic Publishing
Wichita, KS

The 22 Session Plans in the

Faith-Filled Catholic Women's Bible Study Program

are based on the content of the inserts found in the

Faith-Filled Catholic Women's Bible

and the lyrics of the songs found on the

Faith-Filled Catholic Women's Bible Music CD

Songs and Artists on the Catholic Women's Bible Music CD

Magnificat
Words (adapt. From Lk 1:46-55) and music by Lori True;
©2005 GIA Publications, Inc.

What Have We Done for the Poor Ones
Words and music by Lori True;
©2005 GIA Publications, Inc.

Stand Firm
Words and music by Donna Peña;
©1996 GIA Publications, Inc.

One Lord
Words (adapt. from Eph 4) and music by Lori True;
©2005 GIA Publications, Inc.

Forgive Them, Forgive Us
Words and music by Carla J. Giomo;
©2003 GIA Publications, Inc.

The Grail Prayer
Words by The Grail Prayer, trad.
Music by Margaret Rizza; ©1998 Kevin Mayhew Ltd. Admin.
and sub-published in N. America by GIA Publications, Inc.

The Goodness of the Lord
Words (based on Psalm 34) and music by Donna Peña;
©1996 GIA Publications, Inc.

Blessed
Words and music by Susan J. Paul;
©2002 GIA Publications, Inc.

River of Hope
Words and music by Susan J. Paul;
©2002 GIA Publications, Inc.

I Say Yes, Lord/Digo Sí, Señor
Words and music by Donna Peña;
©1989 GIA Publications, Inc.

On that Day
Words and music by Kate Cuddy;
©2001 GIA Publications, Inc.

A Place at the Table
Words by Shirley Erena Murray;
©1998 Hope Publishing Co., Carol Stream, IL 60188 (ASCAP)
All rights reserved. Used with permission. Music by Lori True;
©2002 GIA Publications, Inc.

The Lord is Kind and Merciful
Words (Adapt.from Psalm 103) and
music by Jeanne Cotter;
©1993 GIA Publications, Inc.

In Love We Choose to Live
Words (inspired from 1 Cor:13) and
music by Jeanne Cotter;
©1993 GIA Publications, Inc.

Sanctum nomen
Words and music by Margaret Rizza;
©Kevin Mayhew Ltd. Admin. and sub-published in North
America by GIA Publications, Inc.

Peace, Be Not Anxious
Words by Mary Louise Bringle; ©2002 GIA Publications, Inc.
Music by Lori True ©2005 GIA Publications, Inc,

Calm Me, Lord
Words by David Adam; ©SPCK, Holy Trinity Church,
Marylebone Road, London NW1 4DU. Used by permission
from "The Edge of Glory."
Music by Margaret Rizza;
©1998 Kevin Mayhew Ltd. Admin. and sub-published
in North America by GIA Publications, Inc.

Shadows Gather, Deep and Cold
Words by Sylvia Dunstan; 1995 GIA Publications, Inc.
Music by Kathy Powell; ©2000 GIA Publications, Inc.

If Jesus Wept
Words by Martin Willett
Music by Carol Browning
©2002 GIA Publications, Inc.

My Soul, Triumphant in the Lord (Early American Hymn)
Words by Philip Doddridge
Music by J. Burditt, arr. Alice Parker
Arrangement ©1999 GIA Publications, Inc.

We Will Remember
Words and music by Susan J. Paul;
©2002 GIA Publications, Inc.

Benediction (Let the Mind of Christ Be With You)
Words (based on Phil 2:5) and
music by Carol Browning;
©1999 GIA Publications, Inc.

TABLE OF CONTENTS

Session	Theme	Bible Insert	Song Title	Composer	Page
1	Acceptance	A	Magnificat	Lori True	14
2	Compassion	B	What Have We Done for the Poor Ones	Lori True	19
3	Diligence	C	Stand Firm	Donna Peña	25
4	Faith	D	One Lord	Lori True	29
5	Forgiveness	E	Forgive Them, Forgive Us	Carla J. Giomo	33
6	Generosity	F	The Grail Prayer	Margaret Rizza	39
7	Goodness	G	The Goodness of the Lord	Donna Peña	43
8	Holiness	H	Blessed	Susan J. Paul	47
9	Hope	I	River of Hope	Susan J. Paul	51
10	Humility	J	I Say Yes, Lord/Digo Sí, Señor	Donna Peña	55
11	Joy	K	On that Day	Kate Cuddy	59
12	Justice	L	A Place at the Table	Lori True	65
13	Kindness	M	The Lord Is Kind and Merciful	Jeanne Cotter	71
14	Love	N	In Love We Choose to Live	Jeanne Cotter	75
15	Loyalty	O	Sanctum nomen	Margaret Rizza	79
16	Patience	P	Peace, Be Not Anxious	Lori True	83
17	Peace	Q	Calm Me, Lord	Margaret Rizza	87
18	Sacrifice	R	Shadows Gather, Deep and Cold	Kathy Powell	91
19	Suffering	S	If Jesus Wept	Carol Browning	95
20	Triumph	T	My Soul, Triumphant in the Lord	Arr. Alice Parker	99
21	Understanding	U	We Will Remember	Susan J. Paul	103
22	Wisdom	V	Benediction	Carol Browning	107

Program Overview

The "Faith-Filled Catholic Women's Bible Study Program" consists of 22, ninety-minute sessions. They are designed to enable Catholic women to explore, in a small group setting, the relevance of Scripture to the daily practice of their faith.

Based on the themes of the <u>Faith-Filled Catholic Women's Bible,</u> each session features a creative warm-up activity, interesting questions for group discussion, insightful application of Scripture and inspirational opportunities for both individual and group prayer. The flexible session schedule is designed to avoid the busiest months for families to enhance participation while still complementing the seasons of the Liturgical year.

Session Plan Features:

Thematic Approach - Each session is dedicated to addressing one of the 22 themes of the <u>Faith-Filled Catholic Women's Bible</u>. Themes include Acceptance, Compassion, Diligence, Faith, Forgiveness, Generosity, Goodness, Holiness, Hope, Humility, Joy, Justice, Kindness, Love, Loyalty, Patience, Peace, Sacrifice, Suffering, Triumph, Understanding and Wisdom.

Faith-Filled Catholic Women's Bible Music CD - Each session features the inclusion of a song appropriate for the theme. Produced in cooperation with GIA Publications, Inc., the accompanying Faith-Filled Catholic Women's Bible Music CD is a collection of 22 songs all composed by women.

Opening and Closing Prayers – Each session includes inspirational texts designed to open and close the sessions in prayer. Some sessions include traditional Catholic settings as well as formats for spontaneous prayer.

Spiritual Awakening – The participants are led through a variety of opportunities as a group and as individuals to recognize, reflect and respond to the Word of God. Additional Scripture for personal reading and reflection is also included.

Discussion Questions – Through the creative articles or related Scripture, the participants are drawn into the subject of each session with a series of thought-provoking questions designed to foster lively discussion and/or contemplation.

Group Prayer – As a cornerstone of each session, participants are encouraged to pray together. A structured approach is complemented by an opportunity for each participant to offer personal prayers, praises, thanksgivings and petitions.

Participant's Worksheet – Designed to increase the comfort level and to give every member of the group time to pray and reflect on the themes in advance of the sessions, this handy worksheet includes every question that will be asked at the upcoming session. A personal challenge to respond to Scripture in a practical way, as well as additional verses that any woman can turn to during personal Bible reading, will allow each participant the opportunity to make what started as a group experience truly her own.

A Leader's Guide for Implementation

General Considerations

The Faith-Filled Catholic Women's Bible Study Program Session Plans are written for a facilitator (identified as "Leader" throughout the plans) to use as a guide for small group discussion. This "leadership role" may be held by the same person from week to week or may rotate to other members of the group. Regardless of how this is handled (depending on the dynamics and experience of the members of each group) some considerations for the leader should remain in focus to ensure the success of the program.

Setting - Whether conducted at the church or in homes, the setting for each session is very important. Strive for informality to enhance the experience for all participants. Being able to see each other (with no one apart from the group) is important for many of the activities. The ability to adjust the lighting and maintain convenient access to the CD player is also important. Every effort should be made to create an atmosphere of inclusion. Unlike traditional Bible study that may emphasize lecture and note taking, this experience should be about sharing with each other, both verbally and emotionally.

Preparation - The leader should always be well prepared. Reading over the "Leader's Guide for Group Discussion" (including all the articles and the related Scripture for each insert) several days ahead of time will ensure that all necessary props and materials are at hand before the session begins. Arrangements for refreshments should be made before the session. The leader should always make sure every participant knows the date, time and location of each session.

Participation – It is the leader's responsibility to ensure that each participant has an equal opportunity to participate in every session. This may involve soliciting a response from time to time from someone who is rather shy or quiet or even making sure the discussion and sharing is not dominated by one or two of the strongest members. It is helpful to stress in the first few meetings that the sessions are designed for all to participate where and when they are comfortable doing so. The wording of most of the questions and the supporting language on the Participant's Worksheet stress the importance of everyone being a part of the discussion. However, only the leader can best control what actually happens.

Schedule – **For the Program** - The 22 sessions of the Faith-Filled Catholic Women's Bible Study Program are designed so they can be conducted in any order and at any time of the year. This flexibility allows parishes the opportunity to work this program around busy parish or personal calendars. However, for those groups that can follow it, the accompanying syllabus and suggested schedule facilitates the emphasis of each theme at the most fitting times of the liturgical year. **For the Sessions** – Each session is designed to last 1 hour, 15 minutes. An additional 15 minutes is suggested for fellowship after the session is completed. For convenience and as a tool for the leader to use in keeping the session on schedule, each discussion or activity is listed with a time limit for completion. Because they are only suggestions, the leader may use her discretion to allow for more or less time depending on the response of the participants to that particular discussion or activity. Every effort should be made to give each activity or discussion an appropriate amount of time and to begin and conclude each session on time.

A Leader's Guide for Using the Session Plans

Each of the 22 ninety minute Session Plans contains some elements drawn from the information on the corresponding thematic inserts in the <u>Faith-Filled Catholic Women's Bible</u>. It is critical that each member have a copy of this Bible in hand at each of the sessions. Depending on the theme, some additional elements and/or activities (not found in the <u>Faith-Filled Catholic Women's Bible</u>) may be used to enhance the experience for all participants. Following are the details and some explanation of the resources you will find in this book to support your use of this exciting new program.

Leader's Guide for Group Discussion – The "Leader's Guide for Group Discussion" for each session is designed for use by the **"Leader only."** These pages contain directions for the leader to give and instructions for the leader to follow in accomplishing tasks for the group during each session. In fact, **some plans include exact language for the Leader to use at specific times. At these times, you will find the word "Leader" bolded in front of this text and the exact words underlined.**

Content Descriptions

Title(s) – Each "Leader's Guide for Group Discussion" is clearly titled corresponding to one of the 22 identical titles found on the insert pages of the Faith-Filled Catholic Women's Bible Music CD. The Title bar of each Session Plan also includes the name of the song, composer, CD disc and track location for the corresponding song from the Faith-Filled Catholic Women's Bible Music CD.

Materials Needed - This list contains all the materials that will be needed for that particular session. It is critical that the Leader check this list well in advance of the meeting time to make sure all the participants have what is needed for the session.

Setting the Stage - This reminder for the leader stresses the importance of each participant having a copy of the Participant's Worksheet in advance of the session. It also is a convenient reminder to the leader to follow up as needed with all participants about any change in the meeting date, time or place. The leader is reminded that this is a good time to play the corresponding song on the Faith-Filled Catholic Women's Bible Music CD in the background as one part of enhancing the setting.

Warm Up – This optional activity begins each session to help all the participants focus on one area. Usually directly related to the theme, this activity is valuable in getting the participants to think about the topic of the session in a creative way. Each leader and/or group should decide on the importance, value or need of the warm-up depending on the dynamics of the relationships in the group.

Opening Discussion – The sessions always open (even before prayer) with the sharing of answers to some general questions regarding the theme. These discussions are designed to provide for the smoothest transition from the socializing and fun of the greeting and warm-ups to the more staid atmosphere of personal sharing and prayer. To make them more relevant, when possible, every attempt should be made to adapt these questions to the circumstances in the lives of the participants.

Opening Prayer – The Opening Prayer is always taken from the "**Spiritual Awakening**" section of each insert in the Faith-Filled Catholic Women's Bible. It is important to have each participant join in reading this prayer together. It will ensure that all are on the same page for the next discussion with a focus on the Bible as their primary source for the session.

Spiritual Awakening - Recognizing – At this point in the session plan, the leader is encouraged to ask the participants to volunteer to read and pray together each one of the Scriptures that are printed in the "**Recognizing**" section of "**Spiritual Awakening**." These are some of the Scriptures (not addressed in the lesson plan) that speak to this same theme that are found throughout the Bible. It is important during this part of the session that you create an atmosphere of prayer during the reading of these passages. Reminding all participants that these passages are to be read slowly and that the group will observe some silence between the reading of each passage will help to create this atmosphere. Asking the participants to volunteer any spontaneous acclamations, prayers, praises or thanksgivings that these passages might inspire will also help to emphasize that together they are "praying the Scriptures."

Spiritual Awakening - Reflecting – This section (or sections) provides one of the best opportunities the group will have to do an activity together while sharing their responses with each other. The discussion questions here are designed to encourage each person (and the group as a whole) to reflect on what a specific passage or story and related theme in Scripture means in the context of their lives. It is very important to make sure that all the participants are encouraged and/or have an opportunity to share in these reflections.

Group Prayer – This activity is a cornerstone of the program and very important to the success of each session. In most sessions, there is a Leader's thematic introduction followed by a direction in each prayer for the participants to one-by-one **"enter aloud all individual intentions."** It is important to stress here that these prayers can be petitions, praises or thanksgivings for anything each member has on her heart. The leader should do everything to make this a comfortable and inviting experience. Reminding all from the very first session on that this "Group Prayer" opportunity will be a part of every session will enhance the comfort level for all.

Closing Prayer – In most cases, text is provided for the closing prayer. However, in some instances, reflections on an article, listening to music or even silence may have been chosen as the format for this experience. Again, maintaining a prayerful atmosphere is key to the success of each session.

Fellowship – Each session ends with a reminder of the importance of fellowship and sharing. Arrangements should be made in advance for any refreshments that might be a part of this important activity. Music is always encouraged as a background to this final time together.

Participant's Worksheet - A Participant's Worksheet is designed to increase the comfort level and to give every member of the group time to pray and reflect on the themes in advance of the sessions. This handy worksheet includes every question that will be asked at the upcoming session. A challenge to respond to Scripture in a practical way as well as additional verses to turn to during Bible reading also personalizes the piece for each participant.

Guidelines for Instituting a Women's Bible Study Program in Your Parish

1. Call to Action

It is important for the Pastor or other appropriate leader to articulate the benefits of a Bible Study Program to the parish. Ideally, this should be done both at Mass and through parish media outlets including the weekly bulletin, the parish website or any fliers and/or handouts designed to announce the program.

Among other benefits, a small-group Bible Study Program will . . .
- increase the knowledge of and appreciation for Scripture for participants
- create an opportunity for a faith-based sharing experience outside of weekly Mass
- enhance the sense of community in the parish
- stress the relevance of the lessons in Scripture to everyday life

The Fireside Faith-Filled Catholic Women's Bible Study Program is ideal for use because it . . .
- facilitates meaningful interaction between women in the parish
- promotes a personal relationship with God through a focus on Scripture and prayer
- provides a format to discover the beauty and power of spontaneous prayer

2. Getting Started

Once parish-wide benefits and objectives have been clearly identified and articulated, the following steps will be important to take before instituting a program.

- **Determine the level of interest in the parish** - This could be done through a sign-up sheet (either physically or on-line) over a period of a couple of weeks. The sample "Bulletin Announcement" (A) and "Sign Up Form" (B) would be effective tools to use.

- **Identify the leadership team** - The discussion format for group Bible Study is only as effective as the people who volunteer to be leaders. Spirituality, the ability to work well with people and organizational skills are all very important considerations when selecting a leader. The enclosed "Tips in Selecting Discussion Group Leaders" (C) be helpful in this process.

- **Create and set the schedule** - In creating a schedule for small group study sessions, special care should be taken to choose meeting places that are comfortable and conducive to sharing. Ideally, the schedule should include the opportunity for groups to meet at varying times of the day and on varying days of the week. Giving potential participants several choices is likely to increase participation in the program. The Faith-Filled Catholic Women's Bible Study program includes a Suggested Syllabus and Session Calendar for the 2006-2007 Liturgical Year. However, the program and this proposed schedule are both flexible enough to allow for adjustments due to parish and/or community activities.

3. Conducting the Program

Encouraging testimonials from participants once the program begins is a good way to remind potential participants of the value of joining a discussion group when the opportunity arises throughout the year. Adding new members is especially easy with the "Faith-Filled Catholic Women's Bible Study Program" by utilizing the four breaks that occur between the sessions. Leadership meetings during these breaks also allow for the sharing of successes and any additional training that may be needed.

A. Sample Bulletin Announcement:

There is a sign-up sheet in the <u>Location of Sign Up Sheet</u> for any women in the parish who would be interested in exploring how the lessons in the Bible relate to our everyday lives. Through the sharing of experiences with other women in a small group discussion setting, this program will address themes that will resonate with women. With prayer as it's cornerstone, you'll find this creative program convenient and rewarding. We need to know how many women may be interested in participating before a schedule can be published. For more information or if you have questions about this program, please contact the parish office or call:<u> Contact Person </u>.

B. Sample Sign-up Form:

_____ Yes, I am interested in participating in a Women's Bible Study Group.

Name: _____

The best Day of the Week for me to participate is: _____

The best time of the day for me to participate is: _____

I would be interested in serving as a Group Leader.

_____Yes _____ No

_____ I need to know more information about the program before I decide.

The best time to contact me is:

_____ Daytime _____ Evening _____ Via e-mail

My daytime phone: _____

My evening phone: _____

My e-mail address: _____

C. Tips for Selecting Effective Group Leaders

1. Choose women who express an interest in this role. "Recruiting" women who do not feel comfortable in serving as the leader (although sometimes necessary) should not be the first strategy in building the leadership team.

2. The leader must be spiritually strong. Her focus on God's presence in the discussions as well as her focus on the importance of prayer in responding to Him will help the group to grow.

3. Make sure the women who are selected are willing and able to dedicate the time needed to meet with other leaders and to plan and prepare for the success of each session.

4. Choose women who have experience in working with people. The leader should have the skill to encourage participation from someone who might not be comfortable sharing her thoughts with the group. At the same time, each leader will need to make sure that one or two individuals with stronger personalities do not dominate the discussion in every session.

5. Choose women who are organized and good time managers. Keeping the sessions moving (depending on the response in each section) is important in creating a meaningful experience for all the participants.

6. A leader must be flexible. Events in the parish or in the personal lives of each of the participants might allow for a discussion related to the theme that is "not in the plan." Sometimes the best results in any given discussion can come about because the leader allowed the discussion to take a new direction. Keep in mind, the session plans in the "Faith-Filled Catholic Women's Bible Study Program" are only suggestions.

Suggested Syllabus and Session Calendar

This schedule organizes the 22 sessions into an order of presentation around the seasons of the Liturgical year. For convenience, special care has been taken to avoid scheduling sessions during the traditionally busiest family times of the year including the weeks surrounding holidays and the beginning and ending of the school terms. Meeting times and locations can vary on a parish by parish or even group by group basis.

The Fall Sessions - The five sessions that open the program focus on topics that are inherently meaningful to women. As mothers, daughters, wives and friends, these themes will resonate with all women enhancing both the comfort level of each participant and the cohesiveness and dynamics of each group.

Fall:	Love	September
	Kindness	September
	Generosity	October
	Goodness	October
	Justice	October

The Advent Sessions – These five sessions address themes that are in focus during the Advent Season. With a Scriptural focus on The Blessed Virgin Mary, many of these sessions will give women meaningful yet practical advice on how to open their hearts and minds to the will of God in their lives. The material discussed in these sessions complements the themes of the Scripture proclaimed in this holy season and in unison with it, celebrates the Joy we experience in welcoming Christ into our hearts everyday.

Advent	Acceptance	November
	Patience	December
	Joy	December
	Humility	December

The Winter Sessions – With a focus on the "practice" of faith, these themes allow for a comfortable transition from the busy holiday season to this more predictable season of the new year. The questions and discussions in these sessions will facilitate personal and group reflection on what it means to be a practicing Catholic fostering a deeper and fuller appreciation and understanding of the importance of Faith, Peace and Holiness in our lives.

Winter	Faith	January
	Peace	January
	Holiness	February

The Lenten Sessions – Reflecting the themes of Lent, here are five sessions that will bring each participant and every group face to face with some of the toughest challenges they can face in living a life in imitation of Christ. Drawing heavily from Scripture, through the discussions in these sessions, every woman will discover in herself the depth of her capacity for caring for others and, in so doing, fully realize the depth of God's care and love for her.

Lent	Sacrifice	February
	Forgiveness	February
	Compassion	March
	Suffering	March
	Triumph	March

The Spring Sessions – More than bringing the program to a close, these sessions actually explore many of the same challenges and opportunities faced by the Apostles and the early Church. Drawing heavily on the presence of the Holy Spirit in our lives, these sessions will require each participant and each group to open their minds and hearts as they reflect on how they are responding to Christ's call to spread the Good News.

Spring	Diligence	April
	Loyalty	April
	Wisdom	April
	Hope	May
	Understanding	May

The Faith-Filled Catholic Women's Bible Study Program

A Leader's Guide for Group Discussion

Acceptance
Song: "Magnificat"
Disc 1, Track 1

Insert A-1 through A-4
Composer: Lori True
Faith-Filled Catholic Women's Bible Music CD

Materials Needed

Faith-Filled Catholic Women's Bible and Music CD, CD player, Participant's Worksheet, Holy Water, 4 x 6 Index Card each.

Setting the Stage

Before this session, send each member of the group a welcoming message and a copy of the Participant's Worksheet for this session. Also, send a reminder of the date and time of the session as well as directions to the meeting place (if different from the church). To enhance an atmosphere of **Acceptance**, have the song "Magnificat" from the Faith-Filled Catholic Women's Bible Music CD playing in the background when the participants arrive.

Warm Up - Optional (10 minutes)

Give each participant an index card. Ask them to draw both a vertical and a horizontal line through the center of the card dividing it into four equal sections. Then ask them to complete the following.

In the upper left-hand corner, list three things you like to do.
In the upper right-hand corner, list three of your favorite foods.
In the lower left-hand corner, list three things you like to watch on TV.
In the lower right-hand corner, list the place in the world you would most like to see.

Make sure that no one puts her name on the card. As soon as everyone is finished, put all the cards in a hat and have the first participant draw out a card (it cannot be her card if it is, she must put it back and draw another card). Before she reads the details on the card aloud, tell all participants that they are going to be asked to write down (without discussion) who they think each card describes. Ask the first person to draw a card to write the number #1 on the back of the card. She should ask every participant to write the same number (#1) on the back of their Participant's Worksheet. As she reads the answers to the questions written on the front of the card (what three things #1 likes to do, what #1's three favorite foods are; etc.), the other participants try to guess which woman this may be describing. They each write their guess beside the corresponding number on the back of their Participant's Worksheet. Move around the group until the last participant has read the last card. After the first one, each subsequent card should get the next consecutive number written on the back of the card, corresponding with the numbers written on the back of the Participant's Worksheets. Compare answers with each other. Ask if anyone got all the names correct in their list.

Opening Discussion (15 minutes)

To begin the discussion, ask each participant to share with the group her answer(s) to one, or both, of the following questions:

1. What does acceptance mean to you?
2. What does it mean to be accepted?

Ask the participants to offer their reflections on any of the following questions:

3. Have you ever felt totally accepted (or totally unaccepted) by a person or a group?
4. Do you ever have trouble accepting yourself?
5. Do you sometimes have trouble accepting the circumstances in your life that you can't change?

Spiritual Awakening - Opening Prayer

Ask the participants to read together the **Opening Prayer** at the top of insert page A-2.

Spiritual Awakening - Recognizing (5 minutes)

Leader: The Bible tells us about how God accepts us and how He expects us to accept each other. Ask the participants to read aloud each of the **first five** Scripture passages in the **Recognizing** section of **Spiritual Awakening** on insert page A-2. Remind them to pause for a few seconds in silence after each passage to allow anyone to offer any spontaneous thought, prayer, praise or thanksgiving that this Scripture might inspire. Then, in recognition of the example she set for full acceptance of God's will, conclude this section by all reciting Luke 1:38 followed by praying the Hail Mary together.

Mary said, "Behold, I am the handmaid of the Lord. May it be done to me according to your word." Luke 1:38

Spiritual Awakening - 1ˢᵗ Reflection (15 minutes)

Have the participants read the **Faith in Action** article: "Smile Even at Funerals" on insert page A-3. Discuss the answers to the following questions: Are you fully accepting of God's will? How would your life look different if you rejoiced in Luke 1:38?

Spiritual Awakening - 2ⁿᵈ Reflection (15 minutes)

Ask a volunteer to read James 5:9 (Page 1346). Then, read the following: **Leader:** This verse teaches us not to complain about others that you may not be judged. Ask the participants to share some instance recently where they have found themselves complaining in some way about some person or some situation in their family, at work, or in your community? After discussion: **Leader:** Let's pray James 5:9 again asking God for the strength to refrain from complaining about others and the resolve to choose acceptance by focusing only on the positive things about others.

Group Prayer (10 minutes)

Leader: Dearest Jesus, just as Your Blessed Mother accepted the will of the Father, accept our prayers for these special intentions. May Your answers to our group and individual prayers for each other be made clear to us. Guide us to discern Your will with full acceptance as we ask You for: **enter aloud all individual intentions.** In Jesus' name, we pray, Amen.

Closing Prayer (5 minutes)

Leader: You could say that Baptism is the "Sacrament of Acceptance". In Baptism, we are welcomed into the Body of Christ. As we close, come forward and bless yourself with Holy Water as a reminder of God s acceptance of you. After all have come forward, continue with Let us close today by reciting together the Serenity Prayer.

God, grant me the serenity to accept the things I cannot change, courage to change the things I can, and wisdom to know the difference. Amen.

Fellowship (15 minutes)

After the session is completed and while refreshments are served, play softly in the background: "Magnificat" from the Faith-Filled Catholic Women's Bible Music CD.

The Faith-Filled Catholic Women's Bible Study Program
Participant's Worksheet

<u>Acceptance</u>   <u>Insert A-1 through A-4</u>

Mary said, "Behold, I am the handmaid of the Lord.
May it be done to me according to your word." Luke 1:38

You can prepare for the discussions about the theme **Acceptance** by thinking about how you might answer the following questions:

1. What does acceptance mean to me?

2. What does it mean to me to be accepted?

3. Have I ever felt totally accepted (or unaccepted) by any person or any group of people?

4. Do I ever have trouble accepting myself?

5. Do I have trouble accepting the circumstances in my life that I can't change?

Is there an instance recently where I have found myself complaining in some way about some person or some situation in my family, at work, or in my community?

Group Prayer - My intentions for group prayer this week:

Closing Prayer -

God, grant me the serenity to accept the things I cannot change,
courage to change the things I can, and wisdom to know the difference. Amen.

My personal response in Acceptance for this week - Pray a rosary one morning this coming week specifically asking the Blessed Mother for her help in discerning God's will in your life. Share at least one thing you discover with another woman.

Other Scripture on **Acceptance**:

Ephesians 6:7 (Page 1283) * 1 Peter 2:9 (Page 1349)
Romans 12:5 (Page 1223) * Psalms 118:8 (Page 616)

The Faith-Filled Catholic Women's Bible Study Program

A Leader's Guide for Group Discussion

Compassion
Song: "What Have We Done for the Poor Ones?"
Disc 1, Track 2

Insert B-1 through B-4
Composer: Lori True
Faith-Filled Catholic Women's Bible
Music CD

Materials Needed

Faith-Filled Catholic Women's Bible and Music CD, CD player, Participant's Worksheet.

Setting the Stage

Before this session, send any member of the group that may not have been present at the last session the Participant's Worksheet for this session. Also, send a reminder of the date and time of the session as well as directions to the meeting place (if different from the church). To enhance an atmosphere of **Compassion**, have the song "What Have We Done for the Poor Ones" from the Faith-Filled Catholic Women's Bible Music CD playing in the background when the participants arrive.

Warm Up - Optional (10 Minutes)

Using the back of their Participant's Worksheet, have each person answer this question (with no discussion): "If you were going to be stranded on a desert island, and had only 5 minutes advance notice, what one thing would you bring?" After everyone has written her answer down, have each participant share her answer with the group and her explanation for giving that answer.

Then, as a group, discuss the answer to the following question: If all of us found ourselves on this island with only the one item each of us brought, how could we combine and/or share our contribution to either improve our situation or help us to get off of the island? Encourage the participants to share their answers.

Opening Discussion (15 minutes)

Have the participants share their answers to one or both of these questions:

1. What is compassion?
2. What is the difference between compassion and sympathy?

Ask each participant to share an instance when someone showed her compassion.

Spiritual Awakening - Opening Prayer (5 minutes)

Ask a volunteer to read aloud the **Profile in Faith** article, Veronica on the top of insert page B-3. Then, after a brief period of silence, ask the participants to join together in the **Opening Prayer** on the bottom of insert page B-1.

Spiritual Awakening - Recognizing (5 minutes)

Leader: Jesus often spoke about how He was moved with pity or compassion. Ask for volunteers to read aloud each of the Scripture passages in the **Recognizing** section of **Spiritual Awakening** on insert page B-2. Remind the participants that each reader will pause for a few seconds of silence after each passage to allow anyone to offer any spontaneous thought, prayer, praise or thanksgiving that this Scripture might inspire. After the final Scripture is read, ask the group, What else do these Scriptures teach us about **Compassion**? Share and discuss any responses.

Spiritual Awakening - 1ˢᵗ Reflection (15 minutes)

After having a volunteer read aloud the "Story of the Good Samaritan" in Luke 10:29-37 (Page 1112), ask the participants to share their answers to the following questions:

What are the parallels to the story of the Good Samaritan in today's society? Give an example of a recent opportunity you have had to respond to someone in need. What was the situation? How did you respond? If you failed to respond to the person in need, what were your reasons? How did you feel? Share and discuss your answers with each other.

Spiritual Awakening - 2ⁿᵈ Reflection (15 minutes)

Have another volunteer read Matthew 15:32 (Page 1034). Ask the participants to share their thoughts on what this demonstration of compassion by Jesus teaches us about being sensitive to other's needs. How does this lesson apply to us as individuals or as a society?

Group Prayer (5 minutes)

Leader: Let us now pray together for those less fortunate in the world. Lord, open our hearts with compassion today and every day. We ask You today to accept our praises, hear our thanks and answer our prayers for the intentions we voice and for the intentions we keep in our hearts: **enter aloud all individual intentions**. Knowing the compassion of Your Most Blessed Sacred Heart, we ask these things in Your name, Amen.

Music Reflection/Closing Prayer (10 minutes)

Listen to the song: "What Have We Done for the Poor Ones" from the Faith-Filled Catholic Women's Bible Music CD. After a few seconds of silence, have the participants open their Bibles to Psalm 145 on page 631. Then continue with the following prayer:

Leader: Lord Jesus, in Your goodness You taught us by the feeding of the four thousand that we should constantly remain aware of the needs of others in the world around us. Inspire us to respond like the Good Samaritan at every opportunity sharing love and compassion in imitation of You as we pray: (pray antiphon-ally Psalm 145).

Fellowship (15 minutes)

After the session is completed and while refreshments are served, play softly in the background: "What Have We Done for the Poor Ones" from the Faith-Filled Catholic Women's Bible Music CD.

The Faith-Filled Catholic Women's Bible Study Program

Participant's Worksheet

You can prepare for the discussions about the theme **Compassion** by thinking about how you might answer the following questions:

1. What is compassion?

2. What is the difference between compassion and sympathy?

3. Share an instance when someone showed me compassion?

Read Luke 10:29-37 (Page 1112).
What are the parallels to the story of the Good Samaritan in today's society?

What is a recent opportunity I have had to respond to someone in need?

What was the situation? How did I respond?

If I failed to respond to the person in need, what were my reasons? How did I feel?

Read Matthew 15:32 (Page 1034).
What does this demonstration of compassion by Jesus teach us about being sensitive to other's needs?

How does this lesson apply to me as an individual or to us as a society?

Group Prayer - My intentions for group prayer this week:

Music Reflection/Closing Prayer

> **Lord Jesus, in Your goodness You taught us by the feeding of the four thousand that we should constantly remain aware of the needs ·of others in the world around us. Inspire us to respond like the Good Samaritan at every opportunity sharing love and compassion in imitation of You as we pray: (pray antiphonally Psalm 145 on page 630).**

My personal response in Compassion for this week - Sign up with one of your children or another family member or another woman to work a shift at a neighborhood kitchen, homeless shelter or mission for the needy. When there, go out of your way to visit with one of the people in imitation of the Good Samaritan.

Other Scripture on **Compassion**:
Deuteronomy 30-3 (Page 189) * 1 Samuel 23:21 (Page 265) * 2 Kings 13:23 (Page 333)
2 Chronicles 36:15 (Page 403) * Micah 7:19 (Page 969) * Matthew 14:14 (Page 1032)
Matthew 18:33 (Page 1040) * Mark 1:41 (Page 1067) * Mark 9:22 (Page 1078)

The Faith-Filled Catholic Women's Bible Study Program

A Leader's Guide for Group Discussion

Diligence
Song: "Stand Firm"
Disc 1, Track 3

Insert C-1 through C-4
Composer: Donna Peña
Faith-Filled Catholic Women's Bible Music CD

Materials Needed

Faith-Filled Catholic Women's Bible and Music CD, CD player, Participant's Worksheet.

Setting the Stage

Before this session, send any member of the group that my not have been present at the last session the Participant's Worksheet for this session. Also, send a reminder of the date and time of the session as well as directions to the meeting place (if different from the church). To enhance the theme of **Diligence**, have the song "Stand Firm" from the Faith-Filled Catholic Women's Bible Music CD playing in the background when members of the group arrive.

Warm Up - Optional (10 minutes)

Ask each participant to share her answer to this question: If my relationship with God could be made into a movie of a TV series, what would the title and/or the set-up for the program be? After sharing, take a vote on who came up with the most creative title.

Opening Discussion (15 minutes)

Have the participants read the **Plan and Purpose** article on insert page C-1. Then, ask them to share and discuss their answers to the following questions: Can you identify with the words of St. Paul? Do you sometimes feel like you are in a "race?" If so, how would you characterize your "race of faith?" Is it a series of sprints or is it a marathon? Which is more effective? How does being Catholic make our journey unique? Do you think being diligent is a shared experience in faith or is it more personal for you?

Spiritual Awakening - Opening Prayer

Have the participants read together the **Opening Prayer** at the top of insert page C-2.

Spiritual Awakening - Recognizing (10 minutes)

Ask for volunteers to read aloud each of the Scripture passages in the **Recognizing** section of **Spiritual Awakening** on insert page C-2. Remind the participants that each reader will pause for a few seconds of silence after each passage to allow anyone to offer any spontaneous thought, prayer, praise or thanksgiving that this Scripture might inspire. After the final Scripture is read, ask the group: What else do these Scriptures teach us about **Diligence**? Share and discuss why diligence in faith is especially important in today's world.

Spiritual Awakening - 1st Reflection (20 minutes)

Ask a volunteer to read Mark 1:35 (Page 1066). Then, have the participants discuss the following questions: Are you diligent in your prayer? What is the quality of your prayer life? Do you create a special place and time for God each day? Is there a balance between prayers of adoration and thanksgiving and prayers of petition when you pray? Ask each participant to share how she approaches prayer (spontaneous, memorized, scheduled, time of day, etc.) and, as a result, what role prayer plays in her life.

Faith In Action (15 minutes)

Read the **Faith in Action** article "The Hidden Garden" on insert page C-4. After silent reflection, ask each participant her answer to this question: What are some of the weeds (distractions, obstacles, etc.) that grow in our lives that can easily choke out spending time with God?

Group Prayer/Closing Prayer (5 minutes)

Leader: Focused on the importance of prayer and with hearts full of hope, we ask God to accept our praises, hear our thanks and answer our prayers for the intentions we voice and for the intentions we keep in our hearts: **enter aloud all individual intentions.**

Then, all pray together:

**Heavenly Father, give us the diligence we need to live a Christ-like life.
Keep us free from temptation so that our eyes can remain fixed on You.
Through the intercession of St. Jane Frances de Chantal, we ask You to send good people into our lives to show us the way. Keep our minds and hearts open to Your will. In Jesus' name we pray, Amen.**

Fellowship (15 minutes)

After the session is completed and while refreshments are served, play softly in the background: "Stand Firm" from the Faith-Filled Catholic Women's Bible Music CD.

The Faith-Filled Catholic Women's Bible Study Program

Participant's Worksheet

Diligence   Insert C-1 through C-4

You can prepare for the discussions about the theme **Diligence** by thinking about how you might answer the following questions:

1. Can I identify with the words of St. Paul when he describes faith as a "race?"

2. How would I characterize my "race of faith?" Is it a series of sprints or is it a marathon?

3. Which is more effective?

4. How does being Catholic make my journey unique?

5. Is being diligent a shared experience in our Catholic faith or is it more personal for me?

6. Why is diligence in faith especially important in today's world?

Read Mark 1:35 (Page 1066).
Then, be prepared to discuss the following questions as you reflect on your own prayer life.

Am I diligent in my prayer life?

What is the quality of my prayer life?

Do I create a special place and time for God each day?

Is there a balance between prayers of adoration and thanksgiving and prayers of petition when I pray?

Read the Faith In Action article "A Hidden Garden" on insert page C-4.
Then, be prepared to share your answer to this question: What are some of the "weeds" (distractions, obstacles, etc.) that grow in my life that can easily choke out spending time with God?

Group Prayer/Closing Prayer - My intentions for group prayer this week:

Then, all pray together:

> **"Heavenly Father, give us the diligence we need to live a Christ-like life.**
> **Keep us free from temptation so that our eyes can remain fixed on You.**
> **Through the intercession of St. Jane Frances de Chantal, we ask You to send**
> **good people into our lives to show us the way. Keep our minds and hearts open**
> **to Your will. In Jesus' name we pray, Amen."**

My Personal Response in Diligence for this week - Resolve to get up 15 minutes earlier than normal each day this week to spend some additional quiet time alone with the Lord in His Word.

Other Scripture on **Diligence**:

Philippians 3:13-14 (Page 1290) * Proverbs 4:23 (Page 638) * Hebrews 6:10-12 (Page 1329)

Hebrews 12:15 (Page 1338) * Galatians 6:9 (Page 1276) * Exodus 15:26 (Page 71)

2 Peter 1:10 (Page 1355) * Proverbs 27:23 (Page 659) * Isaiah 55:2 (Page 793)

The Faith-Filled Catholic Women's Bible Study Program

A Leader's Guide for Group Discussion

Faith
Song: "One Lord"
Disc 1, Track 4

Insert D-1 through D-4
Composer: Lorie True
Faith-Filled Catholic Women's Bible Music CD

Materials Needed

Faith-Filled Catholic Women's Bible and Music CD, CD player, Participant's Worksheet.

Setting the Stage

Before this session, send any member of the group that my not have been present at the last meeting the Participant's Worksheet for this session. Also, send a reminder of the date and time of the session as well as directions to the meeting place (if different from the church). To enhance the theme of **Faith**, have the song "One Lord" playing in the background when the participants arrive.

Warm Up - Optional (10 minutes)

You will need a cardboard box and 30 pieces of wadded paper. Ask for one volunteer. Tell her to stand near the center of the group and place the empty cardboard box somewhere behind her (but not directly behind her). Place the 30 pieces of wadded paper within reach of the volunteer. Explain to the group that their job is to give clues to the volunteer that will help her to throw the wads into the cardboard box without turning around. Make sure that the box is far enough away to make the task challenging and therefore, the advice from others helpful. Give examples of clues such as, "A little further to the left." Ask the volunteer to reflect on the feeling of having her success dependent on putting total faith in others to achieve it. Keep the activity going to see how many wads of paper the individual can successfully throw into the box. Allow additional participants to toss if time permits. Discuss other observations as a group.

Opening Discussion (10 minutes)

Have the participants read the **Plan and Purpose** article on insert page D-1. Ask the participants to share their answers to the following questions: What comes to mind when you think about the word faith? How important is the Eucharist in the practice of your faith? Why?

Spiritual Awakening - Opening Prayer

Read together the **Opening Prayer** at the bottom of insert page D-1.

Spiritual Awakening - Recognizing (10 minutes)

Ask for volunteers to read aloud each of the Scripture passages in the **Recognizing** section of **Spiritual Awakening** on insert page D-2. Remind the participants that each reader will pause for a few seconds of silence after each passage to allow anyone to offer any spontaneous thought, prayer, praise or thanksgiving that this Scripture might inspire. After the final Scripture is read, ask the group, "What else do these Scriptures teach us about **Faith**?"

Spiritual Awakening (15 minutes)

Read as a group the Story of Abraham and Isaac in Genesis 22:1-19 (Page 26). Then, ask the participants to share their answers to the following questions: What are some times God has challenged you to demonstrate your faith in Him? Can you give an example of how God has rewarded you because of your obedience in faith?

Faith in Action (15 minutes)

Ask the participants to read the **Faith in Action** article "Just Pull the Chord" on insert page D-4. Then, have the participants share with the group their answers to the following question: What is one area in your life in which you might need to pull the chord and trust God for a landing?

Group Prayer (10 minutes)

Leader: Dearest Lord, we ask You to accept our praises, hear our thanks and answer our prayers for the intentions we voice and for the intentions we keep in our hearts: **enter aloud all individual intentions**. We ask this with these words of faith (All pray the Nicene Creed together).

We believe in one God, the Father, the Almighty, maker of heaven and earth, of all that is, seen and unseen. We believe in one Lord, Jesus Christ, the only Son of God, eternally begotten of the Father, God from God, Light from Light, true God from true God, begotten, not made, one in Being with the Father. Through him all things were made. For us men and for our salvation he came down from heaven: by the power of the Holy Spirit he was born of the Virgin Mary, and became man. For our sake he was crucified under Pontius Pilate; he suffered, died, and was buried. On the third day he rose again in fulfillment of the Scriptures; he ascended into heaven and is seated at the right hand of the Father. He will come again in glory to judge the living and the dead, and his kingdom will have no end. We believe in the Holy Spirit, the Lord, the giver of life, who proceeds from the Father and the Son. With the Father and the Son he is worshiped and glorified. He has spoken through the Prophets. We believe in one holy catholic and apostolic Church. We acknowledge one baptism for the forgiveness of sins. We look for the resurrection of the dead, and the life of the world to come. Amen.

Closing Prayer (5 minutes)

Ask the participants to pray together the "Prayer for Faith to St. Joan of Arc" found at the bottom of the **Profile in Faith** article on insert page D-3.

Fellowship (15 minutes)

After the session is completed and while refreshments are served, play softly in the background: "One Lord" from the Faith-Filled Catholic Women's Bible Music CD.

The Faith-Filled Catholic Women's Bible Study Program

Participant's Worksheet

Faith
_____

Insert D-1 through D-4

You can prepare for the discussions about the theme **Faith** by thinking about how you might answer the following questions:

1. What comes to mind when I think about the word faith?

2. How important is the Eucharist in the practice of my faith? Why?

Read Genesis 22:1-19 (Page 26). Be prepared to discuss your answers to the following questions:

When has God ever challenged me to demonstrate my faith in Him?

How has God rewarded me because of my obedience in faith?

Read the **Faith in Action** article "Just Pull the Chord" on insert Page D-4. Prepare to share with the group your answer to this question:

What is one area in your life in which I might need to "pull the chord" and trust God for a landing?

Group Prayer - My intentions for group prayer this week:

Leader: Dearest Lord, we ask You to accept our praises, hear our thanks and answer our prayers for the intentions we voice and for the intentions we keep in our hearts: **enter aloud all individual intentions.** We ask this with these words of faith (All pray the Nicene Creed together).

The Nicene Creed

We believe in one God, the Father, the Almighty, maker of heaven and earth, of all that is, seen and unseen. We believe in one Lord, Jesus Christ, the only Son of God, eternally begotten of the Father, God from God, Light from Light, true God from true God, begotten, not made, one in Being with the Father. Through him all things were made. For us men and for our salvation he came down from heaven: by the power of the Holy Spirit he was born of the Virgin Mary, and became man. For our sake he was crucified under Pontius Pilate; he suffered, died, and was buried. On the third day he rose again in fulfillment of the Scriptures; he ascended into heaven and is seated at the right hand of the Father. He will come again in glory to judge the living and the dead, and his kingdom will have no end. We believe in the Holy Spirit, the Lord, the giver of life, who proceeds from the Father and the Son. With the Father and the Son he is worshiped and glorified. He has spoken through the Prophets. We believe in one holy catholic and apostolic Church. We acknowledge one baptism for the forgiveness of sins. We look for the resurrection of the dead, and the life of the world to come. Amen.

Closing Prayer - Say the "Prayer for Faith to St. Joan of Arc" at the bottom of the **Profile in Faith** insert page 3-D.

My Personal Response in Faith for this week - Place a different belief statement from the Nicene Creed in a prominent place at home or at work. Share and/or discuss that belief with a family member, colleague or friend.

Other Scripture on **Faith**:

Acts 16:31 (Page 1192) * Ephesians 1:13 (Page 1278) * James 2:19 (Page 1344)
Romans 5:1 (Page 1215) * 1 Corinthians 15:14 (Page 1247) * Philippians 3:9 (Page 1290)
Romans 4:13-16 (Page 1214) * Mark 11:22-23 (Page 1081) * Colossians 2:6-7 (Page 1295)

The Faith-Filled Catholic Women's Bible Study Program

Leader's Guide for Group Discussion

Forgiveness
Song: "Forgive Them, Forgive Us"
Disc 1, Track 5

Insert E-1 through E-4
Composer: Carla J. Giomo
Faith-Filled Catholic Women's Bible Music CD

Materials Needed

Faith-Filled Catholic Women's Bible and Music CD, CD player, Participant's Worksheet.

Setting the Stage

Before this session, send any member of the group that may not have been present at the last session the Participant's Worksheet for this session. Also, send a reminder of the date and time of the session as well as directions to the meeting place (if different from the church). To enhance the theme of **Forgiveness**, have the song "Forgive Them, Forgive Us" playing in the background when the participants arrive.

Warm Up - Optional (15 minutes)

Here is an exercise designed to test how forgiving we are. Read through the list of scenarios below (this list is also on the Participant's Worksheet for this session). Ask the participants to individually rank these situations in order from 1 (easiest to forgive) to 6 (most difficult to forgive). When all are completed have each member share her answers with the group. Discuss the differences.

1. You are anxiously awaiting your husband to come home this evening because today is your 12th Wedding Anniversary. Having completely forgotten what date it is, he walks in the same as usual and says nothing about today being significant in any way.

2. A colleague at work inadvertently gets full credit in a company memo for the success of your project. She sees the error as no big deal and does nothing to correct the misunderstanding.

3. One of your children is critically injured when an old man, while speeding, misjudges a curve and crashes into your car. The old man receives a suspended sentence for negligence, his license is revoked for life and he his fined $15,000. Your child's recovery looks promising but could take as much as a year to be complete.

4. You advised your teenage daughter that you don't approve of her going to see a questionable rock group that is coming to town tonight. It sounded last week like you were winning the battle as she quit asking for your permission. Then, she finds out at school that she can get tickets to the concert after all. She tries to call you but your cell phone is off and you won't be home until 7:00. She takes $30 out of the "family emergency cup" and heads out with friends to the concert thinking she'll explain it all to you later.

5. Another woman that you consider a friend is telling others about something that, even though true, is not very complementary about your family. She thinks she is actually doing you a favor by getting the "true story" out so as not to let the rumor mill get out of hand. You think it would be better if things were simply left unsaid.

6. Others pressured a freind's daughter to have an abortion after making a horrible mistake with a young man she just "knew she was in love with." Choosing the abortion was ultimately her decision and she has been haunted by it ever since. Can she forgive yourself?

Opening Discussion (10 minutes)

Together, read aloud the **Plan and Purpose** article on insert page E-1. Then, ask each participant to write her answers to the questions below (using her Participant's Worksheet). Play the song "Forgive Them, Forgive Us" very quietly in the background to help create a peaceful mood.

Is there a wound in any relationship in my life (family member, colleague, friend) that is not healed because of a lack of forgiveness? What was/is my responsibility for the original wrong? What is stopping healing from taking place in this situation? Have I confessed any sin I may have committed?

Ask any member of the group who is comfortable doing so to share her story with the group (After sharing, go immediately into the group prayer).

Group Prayer (5 minutes)

Leader: Dearest Jesus, we ask Your mercy and forgiveness as we contemplate these wounds in our lives. Give us the courage and loving hearts necessary to forgive those who have wronged us and to seek forgiveness of those we have wronged. We ask You to hear our prayer for our special intentions whether named today or kept in our hearts: **enter aloud all individual intentions.** Shower us with Your grace and blessings today and every day. This we ask, in Your name, Amen.

Spiritual Awakening - Opening Prayer

Have the participants read together the **Opening Prayer** at the top of insert page E-2.

Spiritual Awakening #1 - Recognizing (10 minutes)

Ask for volunteers to read aloud each of the Scripture passages in the **Recognizing** section of **Spiritual Awakening** on insert page E-2. Remind the participants that each reader will pause for a few seconds of silence after each passage to allow anyone to offer any spontaneous thought, prayer, praise or thanksgiving that this Scripture might inspire. After the final Scripture is read, ask the group, What else do these Scriptures teach us about **Forgiveness**? Share and discuss any responses.

Spiritual Awakening #2 - Reflecting (15 minutes)

Read as a group the story of the unforgiving servant in Matthew 18:21-35 (Page 1039). Then, ask any volunteers to share with the group about a time when someone forgave them for wronging them in some way.

Faith in Action (15 minutes)

Read the **Faith in Action** article "The Old Rocker" on insert page E-4. Then, ask the participants to share with the group their answer to the following question: Are you hanging on to anything or do you need to remove anything that might be hindering a closer relationship with God and with the people around you?

Closing Prayer (5 minutes)

Pray together an Act of Contrition asking God for forgiveness and for the resolve to amend our lives.

Fellowship (15 minutes)

After the session is completed and while refreshments are served, play softly in the background: "Forgive Them, Forgive Us:" from the Faith-Filled Catholic Women's Bible Music CD.

The Faith-Filled Catholic Women's Bible Study Program
Participant's Worksheet

<u>Forgiveness</u>   Insert E-1 through E-4

You can prepare for the discussions about the theme **Forgiveness** by thinking about how you would answer the following questions:

1. Is there a wound in any relationship in my life (family member, colleague, friend) that is not healed because of a lack of forgiveness?

2. What was/is my responsibility for the original wrong?

3. What is stopping the healing from taking place in this situation?

4. Have I confessed any sin I may have committed?

5. When did someone forgive me for wronging them in some way?

6. Am I hanging on to anything or do I need to remove anything that might be hindering a closer relationship with God and with the people around me?

Group Prayer - My intentions for group prayer this week:

My Personal Response in Forgiveness for this week - Accept God's grace and experience His loving forgiveness through the reception of the Sacrament of Reconciliation this week.

Other Scripture on **Forgiveness**:

Colossians 1:14 (Page 1293) * Mark 2:5 (Page 1067)
Luke 7:47-48 (Page 1106) * Isaiah 1:18 (Page 748) * Matthew 9:5-6 (Page 1021)
Luke 23:34 (Page 1132) * Matthew 18:18 (Page 1039) * Isaiah 43:25 (Page 783)

Scenario's for Forgiveness Warm Up

_____ 1. You are anxiously awaiting your husband to come home this evening because today is your 12th Wedding Anniversary. Having completely forgotten what date it is, he walks in the same as usual and says nothing about today being significant in any way.

_____ 2. A colleague at work inadvertently gets full credit in a company memo for the success of your project. She sees the error as no big deal and does nothing to correct the misunderstanding.

_____ 3. One of your children is critically injured when an old man while speeding, misjudges a curve and crashes into your car. The old man receives a suspended sentence for negligence, his license is revoked for life and he his fined $15,000. Your child's recovery looks promising but could take as much as a year to be complete.

_____ 4. You advised your teenage daughter that you don't approve of her going to see a questionable rock group that is coming to town tonight. It sounded last week like you were winning the battle as she quit asking for your permission. Then, she finds out at school that she can get tickets to the concert after all. She tries to call you but your cell phone is off and you won t be home until 7:00. She takes $30 out of the "family emergency cup" and heads out with friends to the concert thinking she'll explain it all to you later.

_____ 5. Another woman who you consider a friend is telling others about something that, even though true, is not very complementary about your family. She thinks she is actually doing you a favor by getting the "true story" out so as not to let the rumor mill get out of hand. You think it would be better if things were simply left unsaid.

_____ 6. Others pressured a friend's daughter to have an abortion after making a horrible mistake with a young man she just "knew she was in love with." Choosing the abortion was ultimately her decision and she has been haunted by it ever since. Can she forgive yourself?

38

The Faith-Filled Catholic Women's Bible Study Program

A Leader's Guide for Group Discussion

Generosity
Song: "The Grail Prayer"
Disc 1, Track 6

Insert F-1 through F-4
Composer: Margaret Rizza
Faith-Filled Catholic Women's Bible Music CD

Materials Needed

Faith-Filled Catholic Women's Bible and Music CD, CD player, Participant's Worksheet, 1 Non-perishable Food Item, 4" x 6" Index Card each, Pen.

Setting the Stage

Before this session, send any member of the group that may not have been present at the last session the Participant's Worksheet for this session. Also, send a reminder of the date and time of the session as well as directions to the meeting place (if different from the church). To enhance the theme of **Generosity**, have the song "The Grail Prayer" playing in the background when the participants arrive.

Warm Up Optional (15 minutes)

Arrange the participants in a circle as much as possible. Ask each person to put her name on the top of a 4" x 6" index card. As soon as all are finished, ask everyone to pass their card to the person on their right. This person then writes on the card (in as few words as possible) how they think the person whose name appears at the top of the card exhibits generosity. When all are finished, each member passes the card to the next person on the right and that person writes another way they think that this person (whose name appears at the top of the card) exhibits generosity. No one can duplicate an answer that is already on the card when they receive it. Continue passing the cards to the right until each card returns the person whose name appears at the top of the card. Have each participant share with the group what is written on her card.

Opening Discussion (10 minutes)

Have everyone read the **Faith in Action** article "A Lifetime Lesson" on insert page F-3. When finished, discuss their answers to the following questions: What does the author of this article mean by giving out of our need not just out of our surplus? Why is that so important? Ask the participants to discuss their thoughts on the phenomenon of why it is that often people in the most need are the most generous.

Spiritual Awakening - Opening Prayer

Invite everyone to read together the **Opening Prayer** at the top of insert page F-2.

Spiritual Awakening - Recognizing (5 minutes)

Have the participants read (as a group) each of the Scriptures in the **Recognizing** section of **Spiritual Awakening** on insert page F-2. Remind the participants that each reader will pause for a few seconds of silence after each passage to allow anyone to offer any spontaneous thought, prayer, praise or thanksgiving that this Scripture might inspire. After the final Scripture is read, ask the group, "What else do these Scriptures teach us about **Generosity**?"

Spiritual Awakening - Reflecting (15 minutes)

As a group, read the story of Abigail in 1 Samuel 25:2-43 (Page 266). Ask the participants to share with the group a time in their life when generosity brought about healing and reconciliation. Discuss what other lessons the story of Abigail teaches us?

Spiritual Awakening - Reflecting (15 minutes)

Read Romans 12:6-8 (Page 1223). Then, ask each participant to identify for the group a gift or talent she thinks God has given her. Discuss how God may be asking each of us in this Scripture to share our talents and gifts with each other, with the church, with the community or in society at large. How is sharing our talents a form of generosity?

Group Prayer (10 minutes)

Leader: Heavenly Father, we praise You and adore You. We recognize Your loving generosity in the people, and gifts You have given us. In that same spirit of generosity, we ask You to accept our praises, hear our thanks and answer our prayers for the intentions we voice and for the intentions we keep in our hearts: **enter aloud all individual intentions**. We ask this in Jesus' name, Amen.

Closing Prayer (5 minutes)

Each participant should now hold the item they have brought to donate to the needy.

Leader: Dear friends, our generosity is a reflection of God's generosity to us. We end our session today by bringing forth a small token of our thanks to God and our recognition of the need for generous spirits in today's world. As we bring our item forward to place in the box or basket, we each offer a simple prayer of thanksgiving to you. **After each member brings her item forward and says a spontaneous prayer of offering and or thanksgiving, all respond: "We Thank You, Lord."**

The basket of food can be donated to the parish food pantry,
the community food pantry or to a needy family in the community.

Fellowship (15 minutes)

After the session is completed and while refreshments are served, play softly in the background: "The Grail Prayer" from the Faith-Filled Catholic Women's Bible Music CD.

The Faith-Filled Catholic Women's Bible Study Program

Participant's Worksheet

Generosity   Insert F-1 through F-4

You can prepare for the discussions about the theme **Generosity** by thinking about how you might answer the following questions:

1. What does it mean to give out of our need, not just out of our surplus? What would be an example of both?

2. Why is giving out of need so important?

3. Why is it that often, the people who are in the most need are the most generous? Do I know a person who exhibits this behavior?

Read 1 Samuel 25:2-43 -The story of Abigail (Page 266).

Has there been a time in my life when generosity brought about healing or reconciliation?

What other lessons does this story teach us?

Read Romans 12:6-8 (Page 1223).

How is sharing our gifts and talents a form of generosity?

Group Prayer - My intentions for group prayer this week:

Closing Prayer - Bring a donation of one perishable food item to the group session this week.

Leader: Dear friends, our generosity is a reflection of God's generosity to us. We end our session today by bringing forth a small token of our thanks to God and our recognition of the need for generous spirits in today's world. As we bring your item forward to place in the box or basket, we each offer a simple prayer of thanksgiving to you **(After each member brings her item forward and says a spontaneous prayer of offering and/or thanksgiving, all respond: "We Thank You, Lord.").**

My Personal Response in Generosity for this week - Do something this week for someone you know that cannot possibly repay you. In the spirit of loving generosity, do it anonymously eliminating any worldly recognition or reward for your effort.

Other Scripture on **Generosity**:

Proverbs 14:21 (Page 646) * Proverbs 11:24-25 (Page 643) * Proverbs 28:27 (Page 660)
2 Corinthians, Chapters 8 and 9 (Page 1260) * 1 Timothy 6:18 (Page 1312)

The Faith-Filled Catholic Women's Bible Study Program

A Leader's Guide for Group Discussion

Goodness
Song: "The Goodness of the Lord"
Disc 1, Track 7

Insert G-1 through G-4
Composer: Donna Peña
Faith-Filled Catholic Women's Bible Music CD

Materials Needed

Faith-Filled Catholic Women's Bible and Music CD, CD player, Participant's Worksheet, 1 Roll of Toilet Paper.

Setting the Stage

Before this session, send any member of the group that may not have been present at the last session the Participant's Worksheet for this session. Also, send a reminder of the date and time of the session as well as directions to the meeting place (if different from the church). To enhance the theme of **Goodness**, have the song The "Goodness of the Lord" playing in the background when the participant's arrive.

Warm Up - Optional (10 minutes)

Without saying why, nonchalantly unroll some paper from a toilet tissue roll (3 or 4 squares) and place it in front of you. Pass the roll to the right and ask the participants to each take "some" paper from the roll and put it in front of them. (Do not indicate how much paper to take off the roll or let them discuss or decide together.) When everyone has some paper in front of them and the roll is returned to you, advise the group that for every square of toilet paper that each one has in front of them they have to tell the group one good thing God has done for them in their lives. Ask for a volunteer to begin and move around the room until all have participated. Discuss your answers.

Opening Discussion (15 minutes)

Ask the participants to discuss their answers to the following questions: What small things can we do to make ourselves more conscious of God's goodness? How does our culture and society hide the fact that God is the source of all goodness?

Spiritual Awakening - Opening Prayer

Ask the participants to read together the **Opening Prayer** at the top of insert page G-2.

Spiritual Awakening - Recognizing (10 minutes)

Ask for volunteers to read aloud each of the Scripture passages in the **Recognizing** section of **Spiritual Awakening** on insert page G-2. Remind the participants that each reader will pause for a few seconds of silence after each passage to allow anyone to offer any spontaneous thought, prayer, praise or thanksgiving that this Scripture might inspire. After the final Scripture is read, ask the group, "What else do these Scriptures teach us about **Goodness**?" Share and discuss any responses.

Spiritual Awakening - Reflecting (15 minutes)

Ask a volunteer to read aloud **Genesis 1:1** as a guided reflection. Encourage the participants to relax even closing their eyes to focus on the wonder and power of these events. Discuss how and why these events in the first creation story reflect the essence of what God Himself calls good?

Faith in Action (15 minutes)

Ask for another volunteer to read aloud the **Faith in Action** article "A Gift of Goodness" on insert G-4. When finished, discuss the following question: How is God's goodness revealed in times of extreme challenge or disaster? Ask each participant if there is some experience in their past where goodness came out of what could have been only a bad situation (i.e.; accidents, family problems or challenges, career or job changes, etc.).

Group Prayer (5 minutes)

Leader: O God, in Your goodness, You are the source of all things. We ask You to shower us with Your grace and goodness in answer to our intentions today. Accept our praises, hear our thanks and answer the prayers we voice and the intentions we keep in our hearts: **enter aloud all individual intentions**. Continue to bless us and help us see Your goodness everyday. In Jesus' name we pray, Amen.

Closing Prayer (5 minutes)

Leader: Please turn to page 611 and read antiphonally Psalm 107 as our closing prayer today. We will all read verses 1-3 then alternate on sets I through V.

Fellowship (15 minutes)

After the session is completed and while refreshments are served, play softly in the background: "The Goodness of the Lord" from the Faith-Filled Catholic Women's Bible Music CD.

The Faith-Filled Catholic Women's Bible Study Program

Participant's Worksheet

Goodness   Insert G-1 through G-4

You can prepare for the discussion about the theme **Goodness** by thinking about how you would answer the following questions:

1. What small things can I do to make myself more conscious of God's goodness?

2. How does our culture and society hide the fact that God is the source of all goodness?

3. How do the events in the first Creation Story reflect the essence of what God Himself calls good?

4. How is God's goodness revealed in times of extreme challenge or disaster?

Is there some experience in my past where goodness came out of what could have been only a bad situation (i.e.; accidents, family problems or challenges, career or job changes, etc.)?

Group Prayer - My intentions for group prayer this week:

Closing Prayer -

Leader: Please turn to page 611 and read antiphonally Psalm 107 as our closing prayer today. We will all read verses 1-3 then alternate on sets I through V.

My Personal Response in Goodness for this week - Write or call someone in your life who has been especially good to you. Tell them how much it has meant to you - even if it happened years ago. The effects of goodness last forever.

Other Scripture on **Goodness**:

Exodus 18:9 (Page 74) * Numbers 10:32 (Page 133) * Psalm 23:6 (Page 560)
Jeremiah 31:12 (Page 834) * Psalm 27:13 (Page 562) * Jeremiah 33:9 (Page 838)

The Faith-Filled Catholic Women's Bible Study Program

A Leader's Guide for Group Discussion

Holiness   Insert H-1 through H-4
Song: "Blessed"   Composer: Susan J. Paul
Disc 1, Track 8   Faith-Filled Catholic Women's Bible Music CD

Materials Needed

Faith-Filled Catholic Women's Bible and Music CD, CD player, Participant's Worksheet, Catechism of the Catholic Church.

Setting the Stage

Before this session, send any member of the group that may not have been present at the last session the Participant's Worksheet for this session. Also, send a reminder of the date and time of the session as well as directions to the meeting place (if different from the church). To enhance an atmosphere of **Holiness,** have the song "Blessed" from the Faith-Filled Catholic Women's Bible Music CD playing in the background when the participants arrive.

Warm Up - Optional (15 minutes)

Ask the participants to take a few minutes to think about one person that they would consider "holy." This could be a famous person or someone as inconspicuous as the woman sitting next to them. It might be a family member or someone who lives far away. This person might be alive today or they might be a person from the past. The challenge for each participant is that, when they are ready, they must introduce the subject they chose to the rest of the group as "a holy person." This will involve explaining why each participant feels their subject qualifies, what it is about them that sets them apart, etc. After the introductions, segue into the opening discussion.

Opening Discussion (15 minutes)

Ask the participants to discuss their answers to the following questions: What does it mean to be holy? How does one live a "holy life?" Is holiness something you consciously strive for . . . . or do you think holiness is reserved for the saints?

Spiritual Awakening - Opening Prayer

Have the participants read together the **Opening Prayer** at the top of insert page H-2. Ask for volunteers to read aloud each of the Scripture passages in the **Recognizing** section of **Spiritual Awakening** on insert page H-2. Remind the participants that each reader will pause for a few seconds of silence after each passage to allow anyone to offer any spontaneous thought, prayer, praise or thanksgiving that this Scripture might inspire. After the final Scripture is read, ask the group: What else do these Scriptures teach us about holiness?

Spiritual Awakening - Reflecting (15 minutes)

Read the Catechism of the Catholic Church, Paragraph 2015. Then, ask a volunteer to read 2 Timothy 4:1-18 (Page 1316). Ask each participant to share her answers to the following questions: What are some obstacles to holiness for you? What plan or tactic should you employ to avoid or rid your life of these obstacles?

Group Prayer (10 minutes)

Leader: Begging the intercession of St. Térèse, the Little Flower, let us offer our petitions to her in the words of the St. Terese Prayer from the **Profile in Faith** article on the bottom of insert page H-3. May God hear our intentions through her and may we be blessed because of it with the flowers of His grace. O Little Therese **enter aloud all individual intentions.** In Jesus' name we pray, Amen.

Closing Prayer (15 minutes)

Ask the participants to read aloud the **Faith in Action** article "You are at the Center" on insert page H-4. Then, in silent reflection, listen to the song Magnificat on Disc 1, Track 1 of the Faith-Filled Catholic Women's Bible Music CD. **Leader:** As you listen, reflect on where your life is centered today. Ask God to confirm your resolve to put Him more at the center of your life and not just on the edge. Pray for an increased devotion to the Blessed Mother to teach you, in her example, how to put Christ at the center. After the song is finished, all pray the Hail Mary together.

Fellowship (15 minutes)

After the session is completed and while refreshments are served, play softly in the background: "Blessed" from the Faith-Filled Catholic Women's Bible Music CD.

The Faith-Filled Catholic Women's Bible Study Program

Participant's Worksheet

You can prepare for the discussions on the theme **Holiness** by thinking about how you might answer the following questions:

1. Who do you consider to be a holy person (past or present)? How would you introduce them emphasizing their holiness?

2. What does it mean to be holy?

3. How does one live a "holy life?"

4. Is holiness something you consciously strive for . . . or do you think it is reserved for the saints?

5. What are some obstacles to holiness for me?

6. What plan or tactic should I employ to avoid or rid my life of these obstacles?

Group Prayer - My intentions for group prayer this week:

My Personal Response in Holiness for this week - Build into your schedule an hour of adoration in front of the Blessed Sacrament this week. Dedicate your prayer and listening during that hour to God's holiness and your desire to share in that holiness in some way.

Other Scripture on **Holiness**:

1 Peter 2:5-10 (Page 1349) * Ephesians 5:27 (Page 1283)
2 Corinthians 7:1 (Page 1259) * Romans 12:1-2 (Page 1223)
Hebrews 12:14 (Page 1338) * 1 Thessalonians 5:23 (Page 1301)

The Faith-Filled Catholic Women's Bible Study Program

A Leader's Guide for Group Discussion

Hope
Song: "River of Hope"
Disc 1, Track 9

Insert I-1 through I-4
Composer: Susan J. Paul
Faith-Filled Catholic Women's Bible Music CD

Materials Needed

Faith-Filled Catholic Women's Bible and Music CD, CD player, Participant's Worksheet, Beanbag or Fabric Ball.

Setting the Stage

Before this session, send any member that may not have been present at the last session the Participant's Worksheet for this session. Also, send a reminder of the date and time of the session as well as directions to the meeting place (if different from the church). To enhance an atmosphere of **Hope**, have the song "River of Hope" from the Faith-Filled Catholic Women's Bible Music CD playing in the background when the participants arrive.

Warm-Up - Optional (15 minutes)

With the participants all within tossing distance of each other, hand a soft beanbag or cloth ball to the first person. Tell them that they are to toss the ball to any other member. When a participant is tossed the ball, she must share with the group something that she considers a hope or dream for herself. Explain that these can be your hopes for yourself, your family or even society in generall. Ask each participant to keep a record on the back of her Participant's Worksheet of what hopes and/or dreams she mentions. Continue tossing the ball until all have had an opportunity to give three answers. (Keep the list for use later in the session).

Opening Discussion (15 minutes)

Have the participants read silently the **Plan and Purpose** article on insert page I-1. After some silent reflection, ask the group to share and discuss their answers to the following questions: What is hope? Do you consider yourself to be a hopeful person? What is the reason for your hope? How does having hope help you deal with challenges including things like pain and suffering?

Spiritual Awakening - Opening Prayer

Invite the participants to pray together the **Opening Prayer** at the top of insert page I-2.

Spiritual Awakening - Recognizing (10 minutes)

Ask for volunteers to read aloud each of the Scripture passages in the **Recognizing** section of **Spiritual Awakening** on insert page I-2. Remind the participants that each reader will pause for a few seconds of silence after each passage to allow anyone to offer any spontaneous thought, prayer, praise or thanksgiving that this Scripture might inspire. After the final Scripture is read, ask the group, "What else do these Scripture verses teach us about **Hope**?" Share and discuss any responses.

Spiritual Awakening - Reflecting (10 minutes)

Read aloud Romans 8:18-25 (Page 1218). Ask the group to look again at the list of hopes and dreams they wrote down in the Warm Up exercise. Have each participant ask themselves: Are my hopes and dreams focused on earthly things? What does this Scripture challenge me to hope for? Share your thoughts with each other.

Faith In Action (15 minutes)

Read together the **Faith in Action** article "Door Number Three" on insert page I-4. Discuss these questions: Can you think of an example of how today's culture pushes for immediate gratification. How are we tempted to "cash in" the immediate rewards on the things we can see over the reward of eternal life that we cannot see. Give an example of how advertising exploits this temptation in our culture.

Group Prayer (5 minutes)

Leader: Heavenly Father, in the spirit of hope, we offer these prayers, praises and petitions to You: **enter aloud all individual intentions**. Accept these prayers along with our silent prayers today and every day. Guide and protect us as we seek continually to hope in You. In Jesus' name we pray, Amen.

Closing Prayer (5 minutes)

Leader: As each participant comes forward, place your hands on their heads and give them the blessing from Romans 15:13: **"May the God of hope fill you with joy and peace in believing, so that you may abound in hope by the power of the Holy Spirit."**

Fellowship (15 minutes)

After the session is completed and while refreshments are served, play softly in the background: "River of Hope" from the Faith-Filled Catholic Women's Bible Music CD.

The Faith-Filled Catholic Women's Bible Study Program

Participant's Worksheet

<u>Hope</u>   <u>Insert I-1 through I-4</u>

You can prepare for the discussions on the theme **Hope** by thinking about how you might answer the following questions:

1. What is Hope?

2. Do I consider myself to be a hopeful person?

3. What is the reason for my hope?

4. How does hope help me deal with my challenges including pain and suffering?

5. Are my hopes and dreams focused on earthly things?

6. What does this Scripture challenge me to hope for?

7. What is an example of how today's culture pushes for immediate gratification?

8. How are we tempted to "cash in" on the rewards of the things we can see over the eternal reward of the things we cannot see?

9. Give an example of how advertising exploits this temptation in our culture.

Group Prayer - My intentions for group prayer this week:

My Personal Response in Hope for this week write or call someone you know who seems to be discouraged or depressed. Let your encouragement be an example to them of how meaningful hope can be in a Christian life.

Other Scripture on **Hope**:

1 John 3:3 (Page 1361) * Psalm 71:14 (Page 588) * Proverbs 23:18 (Page 655)
2 Corinthians 3:12 (Page 1255) * Galatians 5:5 (Page 1275) * Ephesians 1:18 (Page 1278)
2 Thessalonians 2:16-17 (Page 1304) * Titus 2:13 (Page 1320) * Hebrews 3:6 (Page 1327)

The Faith-Filled Catholic Women's Bible Study Program

A Leader's Guide for Group Discussion

Humility
Song: "I Say Yes/Digo Sí Señor"
Disc 1, Track 10

Insert J-1 through J-4
Composer: Donna Peña
Faith-Filled Catholic Women's Bible Music CD

Materials Needed

<u>Faith-Filled Catholic Women's Bible</u> and Music CD, CD player, Participant's Worksheet, Large Bowl of Water, Pitcher and Towels.

Setting the Stage

Before this session, send any member of the group that may not have been present at the last session the Participant's Worksheet for this session. Also, send a reminder of the date and time of the session as well as directions to the meeting place (if different from the church). To enhance an atmosphere of **Humility**, have the song "I Say Yes/Digo Sí Señor" from the Faith-Filled Catholic Women's Bible Music CD playing in the background when the participants arrive.

Warm Up Optional (15 Minutes)

<u>**Leader:** In the beautiful story of Christ's life, the Blessed Virgin Mary gives us the perfect example of the role humility plays in accepting God's will in our lives. Throughout His life and especially in His passion, death and resurrection, Jesus showed us the ultimate example. The seasons of Advent and Lent give us the perfect opportunity to reflect on the importance of humility in a Christian life. As a warm up today, beginning with the letter A, I will ask the person on my right to give me a word associated with either Advent or Lent that begins with that letter A. Then, passing to the person on her right, they must give a word associated with Advent or Lent that begins with the letter B. We will proceed to the right through the alphabet. When someone cannot come up with a satisfactory answer (as judged by the group) she is eliminated and her turn passes to the next person on her right. If we get to the end of the alphabet we start at A again until only one person remains.</u> **Ask for one participant to keep a record of the words used.**

Opening Discussion (15 minutes)

Ask for a volunteer to read the **Plan and Purpose** article on insert page J-1. After some silent reflection, discuss the following questions as a group: What is humility? Is humility praised in our society? Give some examples. Do you ever feel under pressure to keep your relationship with God a secret? Give an example of how we can demonstrate that we believe God is the source of everything in our lives?

Spiritual Awakening - Opening Prayer

Have the participants pray together the **Opening Prayer** at the top of insert page J-2.

Spiritual Awakening - Recognizing (10 minutes)

Ask for volunteers to read aloud each of the Scripture passages in the **Recognizing** section of **Spiritual Awakening** on insert page J-2. Remind the participants that each reader will pause for a few seconds of silence after each passage to allow anyone to offer any spontaneous thought, prayer, praise or thanksgiving that this Scripture might inspire. After the final Scripture is read, ask the group, "What else do these Scriptures teach us about **Humility**?" Share and discuss any responses.

Spiritual Awakening - Reflecting (20 minutes)

Read as a group Mark 9:33-37 (Page 1078). After a pause, have each participant share with the group one time in her life when the Lord taught her a lesson in humility. Discuss as a group the phenomenon of "needing to be first" in our society. Where does this come from? What role does the virtue of humility have in combating this temptation? Discuss how "keeping up with the Jonses" can be prideful. Invite the participants to share about a time when they took credit for a success that was truly God's success through them.

Group Prayer (5 minutes)

Leader: Asking the intercession of St. Rita, who prayerfully bore a painful mark of faith in humble service to the Lord, let us offer our intentions as we pray the Prayer to St. Rita at the bottom of insert page J-3. St. Rita, come to my aid! **Remind the participants that they will be entering their individual intentions one at a time at the appropriate spot in the prayer.**

Closing Prayer (5 minutes)

Have the participants read in silence the article "It Isn't About Me" on insert page J-4. As soon as all are finished, end with this "Prayer of Vocations."

God our Father, in baptism You called us by name and made us members of Your people, the Church. We praise You for Your goodness, we thank You for Your gifts. Father, bless Your Church with love. Raise up dedicated and generous leaders from our families and from our friends who will serve as sisters, priests and brothers. Send Your Spirit to guide and strengthen those You are calling to serve Your people,   following the example of Your Son, Jesus Christ, in whose name we offer this prayer. Amen.

Fellowship (15 minutes)

After the session is completed and while refreshments are served, play softly in the background the song "I Say Yes/Digo Sí Señor" from the Faith-Filled Catholic Women's Bible Music CD.

The Faith-Filled Catholic Women's Bible Study Program

Participant's Worksheet

Humility   Insert J-1 through J-4

You can prepare for the discussions on the theme **Humility** by thinking about how you might answer the following questions:

What is humility?

Is humility praised in our society? Give some examples.

Do I ever feel pressure to keep my relationship with God a secret?

What is one example of how I demonstrate that I believe that God is the source of everything in my life?

Read Mark 9:33-37 (Page 1078).
When was a time in my life when the Lord taught me a lesson in humility?

Where do I think the need to be first comes from in our society? What role does humility play in combating this temptation?

How can keeping up with the Jonses be prideful? Have I ever taken credit for a success that was truly God's success through me?

Group Prayer - My intentions for group prayer this week:

My Personal Response in Humility for this week - Read one of the many books available on the life of Blessed Mother Teresa. As you read, keep notes on the quotes and examples of humility in her life.

Other Scripture on Humility:

Job 5:11 (Page 522) * Psalm 138:6 (Page 627) * Proverbs 18:12 (Page 650)
Proverbs 27:2 (Page 658) * Matthew 20:26-27 (Page 1043) * Luke 18:13-14 (Page 1123)
Ephesians 4:2 (Page 1281) * James 4:6-10 (Page 1345) * 2 Chronicles 34:27 (Page 401)

The Faith-Filled Catholic Women's Bible Study Program

A Leader's Guide for Group Discussion

Joy	Insert K-1 through K-4
Song: "On That Day"	Composer: Kate Cuddy
Disc 1, Track 11	Faith-Filled Catholic Women's Bible Music CD

Materials Needed

Faith-Filled Catholic Women's Bible and Music CD, CD player, Participant's Worksheet, Note Pad (each).

Setting the Stage

Before this session, send any member of the group that may not have been present at the last session the Participant's Worksheet for this session. Also, send a reminder of the date and time of the session as well as directions to the meeting place (if different from the church). To enhance an atmosphere of **Joy**, have the song "On That Day" from the Faith-Filled Catholic Women's Bible Music CD playing in the background when the participants arrive.

Warm Up Optional (15 minutes)

Leader: Finding Joy in our lives is sometimes as simple as being able to laugh at ourselves about the little things that happen to us. Write your answers to these questions on the back of your Participant's Worksheet.

1. Have you ever locked yourself out of the house?
2. Have you ever lost a member of the family while out shopping?
3. Have you ever put something unusual in the refrigerator?
4. Have you ever accidentally turned a load of laundry pink (or another color)?
5. Have you ever left the house and left the iron on?
6. Have you ever put your heel through the hem of a dress?
7. Have you ever had your zipper break in public?
8. Have you ever driven off with something still on top of your car?
9. Have you ever gone somewhere with two different socks or shoes on?
10. Have you ever remembered an appointment after it was too late?
11. Have you ever accidentally called a member of the family by the wrong name?
12. Have you ever been ready to take a bath or shower only to find that you have no hot water?
13. Have you ever fallen up the stairs?
14. Have you ever backed out of the garage only to find the garage door wasn't yet open?
15. Have you ever gone shopping and discovered you didn't bring your purse, wallet or any means to pay?
16. Have you ever driven away from somewhere while someone you brought with you was still standing outside the car?
17. Have you ever dialed a phone number and forgot who you called?
18. Have you ever locked your keys in the car?
19. Have you ever got into the car to go somewhere and forgot where you were going?
20. Have you ever put something in the oven to bake and forgot about it?

Share your answers with each other. To make it even more fun, you could give the person who answered yes to the most questions some kind of spoof prize.

Opening Discussion (15 minutes)

Have each participant share her answers to the following questions: (Discuss each question before moving on to the next question.) What is joy? How is joy related to happiness? How is joy related to peace? How is joy related to service? Ask the participants to share any specific time when they experienced true joy in their lives.

Spiritual Awakening - Opening Prayer

Ask the participants to pray together the **Opening Prayer** at the top of insert page K-2.

Spiritual Awakening - Recognizing (10 minutes)

Ask for volunteers to read aloud each of the Scripture passages in the **Recognizing** section of **Spiritual Awakening** on insert page K-2. Remind the participants that each reader will pause for a few seconds of silence after each passage to allow anyone to offer any spontaneous thought, prayer, praise or thanksgiving that this Scripture might inspire. After the final Scripture is read, ask the group, "What else do these Scriptures teach us about **Joy**?" Share and discuss any responses.

Spiritual Awakening - Reflecting (15 minutes)

As a group, read Matthew 25:14-30 (Page 1053).

After some reflection, have each participant put her name at the top of her pad of paper. Everyone should then pass her pad to the person on the right. Each person then writes one talent or positive characteristic about the person (whose name appears at the top of the pad). Continue passing the pads to the right until each pad is returned to the original owner.

Then, one by one, have each participant read aloud slowly the things that others identified in her as talents or positive characteristics. Discuss reactions. Keep this list for a **Spiritual Awakening - Responding** activity this week.

Group Prayer (5 minutes)

Leader: Heavenly Father, we thank You for the talents and the gifts You give us. Guide us to use them to give You glory in service to each other. With joy and thanksgiving, we pray that You will accept our prayers and praises as well as hear our petitions today as You reveal for us Your answer to questions and challenges in our lives: **enter aloud all individual intentions**. We ask this, in Jesus' name, Amen.

Faith in Action (10 minutes)

Read silently the **Faith in Action** article, "Not a Size Six" on insert page K-4. Answer as a group: What does it mean when someone is radiant in regard to their faith? Is it realistic to expect anyone to be joyful all the time? How does radiance and joy happen in the course of our day to day lives?

Closing Prayer (5 minutes)

Leader: Read together "The Magnificat," a prayer of joy in Luke 1:46-55 (Page 1093).

"My soul proclaims the greatness of the Lord;
my spirit rejoices in God my savior.
For he has looked upon his handmaid's lowliness;
behold, from now on will all ages call me blessed.
The Mighty One has done great things for me,
and holy is his name.
His mercy is from age to age to those who fear him.
He has shown might with his arm,
dispersed the arrogant of mind and heart.
He has thrown down the rulers from their thrones
but lifted up the lowly.
The hungry he has filled with good things;
the rich he has sent away empty.
He has helped Israel his servant, remembering his mercy,
according to his promise to our fathers,
to Abraham and to his descendants forever."

Fellowship (15 minutes)

After the session is completed and while refreshments are served, play softly in the background: "On That Day" from the Faith-Filled Catholic Women's Bible Music CD.

The Faith-Filled Catholic Women's Bible Study Program

Participant's Worksheet

You can prepare for the discussion about the theme **Joy** by thinking about how you would answer the following questions:

1. What is joy?

2. How is joy related to happiness?

3. How is joy related to peace?

4. How is joy related to service?

5. What was a specific time when I experienced true joy in my life?

6. What does it mean when someone is radiant in regard to their faith?

7. Is it realistic to expect anyone to be joyful all the time?

8. How do radiance and joy happen in the course of my day to day life?

Group Prayer - My intentions for group prayer this week:

Group Prayer - The text for "The Magnificat" (Luke 1:46-55) can be found on page 1093.

My Personal Response in Faith for this week - Next week read each day the list the other participants made in the Spiritual Awakening Responding activity of this lesson. Resolve to cultivate the talent or characteristics that you least expected to be on this list. Ask yourself, like the Master in the story of the talents in Matthew 25:14-30 (Page 1053), "Am I giving God good reason to **react with joy** as a result of how I am using my gifts?" "Are there ways that I can do more with the abilities God has given me?"

Other Scripture on **Joy**:

Psalm 47:6 (Page 574) * Isaiah 29:19 (Page 770) * Isaiah 51:11 (Page 790)
Matthew 5:12 (Page 1015) * Luke 1:14, 44 (Page 1092) * John 15:11 (Page 1160)
Acts 13:52 (Page 1188) * Philippians 4:4 (Page 1291) * James 1:2 (Page 1342)

The Faith-Filled Catholic Women's Bible Study Program

A Leader's Guide for Group Discussion

Justice
Song: "A Place at the Table"
Disc 2, Track 1

Insert L-1 through L-4
Composer: Lori True
Faith-Filled Catholic Women's Bible Music CD

Materials Needed

Faith-Filled Catholic Women's Bible and Music CD, CD player, Participant's Worksheet, Candles (1 each), Poster Board.

Setting the Stage

Before this session, send any member of the group that may not have been present at the last session the Participant's Worksheet for this session. Also, send a reminder of the date and time of the session as well as directions to the meeting place (if different from the church). To enhance an atmosphere of **Justice**, have the song "A Place at the Table" from the Faith-Filled Catholic Women's Bible Music CD playing in the background when the participants arrive.

Warm Up - Optional (10 minutes)

Leader: The refrain of the song "A Place at the Table" tells us that it is our responsibility to work for justice wherever injustices exist. For our warm up we are going to play a word game similar to Wheel of Fortune. (Have the blanks set up as below in an easy-to-read format on a large piece of poster board.) Each of us will have alternating opportunities to guess which letters are in these **Words of Injustice**. With each correct guess, write that letter on the appropriate space. If, a person guesses a letter, and that letter is not in the word, the turn moves to the next person. If any person chooses a correct letter, she gets 5 seconds to say the word out loud. If she cannot, then it moves on to the next person. Only the person who selects a correct letter has a chance to solve the puzzle.

__ __ __ __ __ __	F A M I N E
__ __ __ __ __ __ __	P O V E R T Y
__ __ __ __ __ __ __ __	A B O R T I O N
__ __ __ __ __ __ __ __ __	P R E J U D I C E
__ __ __ __ __	C R I M E
__ __ __ __ __ __ __ __ __	I G N O R A N C E
__ __ __ __ __ __ __	D I S E A S E
__ __ __	W A R

Opening Discussion (15 minutes)

Begin by having the participants discuss their answers to the following questions: When you hear the word "justice" what do you think of? Is justice the same as "fairness?" There is a popular saying "If you want peace, work for justice." How is justice related to peace? Ask anyone to volunteer an example from their past of how correcting an injustice in a situation (between family, friends or in the community) helped to bring peace to a situation.

Spiritual Awakening - Opening Prayer

Pray together the **Opening Prayer** at the top of insert page L-2.

Spiritual Awakening - Recognizing (5 minutes)

Ask for volunteers to read aloud each of the Scripture passages in the **Recognizing** section of **Spiritual Awakening** on insert page L-2. Remind the participants that each reader will pause for a few seconds of silence after each passage to allow anyone to offer any spontaneous thought, prayer, praise or thanksgiving that this Scripture might inspire. After the final Scripture is read, ask the group, "What else do these Scriptures teach us about **Justice**?" Share and discuss any responses.

Spiritual Awakening - Reflecting (15 minutes)

Read Luke 16:19-31 (Page 1121). Discuss the following questions in the context of Social Justice. Reflect on your relationship with the disadvantaged in our society - the people like Lazarus. When do you think about them? Why do you think some people forget disadvantaged people? Do you help them? How? Do you pray for them? What person or group of people in your world could be substituted for Lazarus in this story?

Spiritual Awakening Reflecting (15 minutes)

Read Luke 16:19-31 (Page 1121) a second time. Discuss the following questions in the context of God's Justice. Do you think the poor and disadvantaged have a better chance of receiving an eternal reward? Are people of means held to a higher standard in facing God's justice? Discuss how you think we will be judged in relation to our comparative wealth with the rest of the world?

Group Prayer (5 minutes)

Leader: Dearest Jesus, we pray that in Your mercy, we may one day be judged worthy to enter the gates of heaven. Accept our group prayer today with this goal in mind. We praise You, we thank You for blessing our lives. Accept these, praises, prayers and petitions as a visible sign of our faith and our need for Your loving justice: **enter aloud all individual intentions**. In Jesus' name we pray, Amen.

Faith in Action/ Closing Prayer (10 minutes)

Read silently the **Faith in Action** article "The Vacant Lot" on insert page L-4. Discuss as a group what you think some of the "weeds, trash, and pests" in our society are.

After the discussion, have each participant come forward to light a candle and pray silently for God's justice to prevail in each of these problems in our society.

Fellowship (15 minutes)

After the session is completed and while refreshments are served, play softly in the background: "A Place at the Table" from the Faith-Filled Catholic Women's Bible Music CD.

The Faith-Filled Catholic Women's Bible Study Program

Participant's Worksheet

<u>Justice</u>   Insert L-1 through L-4

You can prepare for the discussion about the theme **Justice** by thinking about how you would answer the following questions:

1. When I hear the word "justice" what do I think of?

2. Is justice the same as "fairness?"

3. How is justice related to peace?

4. Have I had an experience in my past where correcting an injustice in a situation (between family, friends or in the community) helped to bring peace to a situation?

Read Luke 16:19-31 (Page 1121). Think about your relationship to the disadvantaged.

When do I think about them?

Why do I think some people forget disadvantaged people?

Do I help them? How? Do I pray for them?

What person or group of people in my world could be substituted for Lazarus in this story?

Do I think that the poor and disadvantaged have a better chance of receiving an eternal reward?

Are people of means held to a higher standard in facing God's justice?

How do I think I will be judged in relation to my comparative wealth with the rest of the world?

Group Prayer - My intentions for group prayer this week:

My Personal Response in Justice for this week - Justice demands that we live righteously so as to earn eternal reward. Resolve to respond justly to a specific obligation or responsibility in your life.

Other Scripture on **Justice**:

Exodus 19:3-6 (Page 74) * Matthew 25:40 (Page 1054) * Matthew 5:43-44 (Page 1016)

Wisdom 8:7 (Page 686) * Romans 3:21-26 (Page 1213) * Luke 9:11-27 (Page 1108)

The Faith-Filled Catholic Women's Bible Study Program

A Leader's Guide for Group Discussion

Kindness

Song: "The Lord is Kind and Merciful"

Disc 2, Track 2

Insert M-1 through M-4

Composer: Jeanne Cotter

Faith-Filled Catholic Women's Bible Music CD

Materials Needed

Faith-Filled Catholic Women's Bible and Music CD, CD player, Participant's Worksheet, Paper, Pen.

Setting the Stage

Before this session, send any member of the group that may not have been present at the last session the Participant's Worksheet for this session. Also, send a reminder of the date and time of the session as well as directions to the meeting place (if different from the church). To enhance an atmosphere of **Kindness**, have the song "The Lord is Kind and Merciful" from the Faith-Filled Catholic Women's Bible Music CD playing in the background when the participants arrive.

Warm Up - Optional (10 minutes)

Beginning with the leader, in order, have each participant tell one nice or complimentary thing they have heard someone else say (or something that is common knowledge among others) about the person to her right. Comments like "She makes the best homemade bread" or "She is the best bridge player" or "She is always so polite to others" etc. If a participant wants to share something about some other member of the group (who does not sit at her right) she may. However, make sure everyone is complimented at least once before the activity is complete. It works best if you go around the group two or three times. Encourage discussion, affirmation and fun.

Opening Discussion (10 minutes)

Have each participant share her answers to the following questions: What does the word kindness mean to you? Tell of a memorable time when someone showed you a kindness. What did they do? How did you feel? How do you think society would be changed if more people treated others with kindness?

Spiritual Awakening - Opening Prayer

Pray together the **Opening Prayer** at the top of insert page M-2.

Plan and Purpose (20 minutes)

Ask a volunteer to read aloud the "Parable of the Good Samaritan" in Luke 10:29-37 (Page 1112). Immediately following the Scripture, read aloud the **Plan and Purpose** article on insert page M-1. After silent reflection, discuss the answers to the following questions: Why is it significant that the first two people who ignored the man in need were a Priest and a Levite? What is symbolic about the fact that it is a Samaritan (someone from outside the mainstream of society) who extended kindness to the man in need? What is a contemporary equivalent to this parable? Why do you think we often react just as the Priest and Levite did when people are in need? Why is just helping a little not enough? Discuss your answers with each other.

Spiritual Awakening - Recognizing (10 minutes)

Ask for volunteers to read aloud the Scripture passages in the **Recognizing** section of **Spiritual Awakening** on insert page M-2. Remind the participants that each reader will pause for a few seconds of silence after each passage to allow anyone to offer any spontaneous thought, prayer, praise or thanksgiving that this Scripture might inspire. After the final Scripture is read, ask the group, "What else do these Scriptures teach us about **Kindness**?" Share and discuss any responses.

Spiritual Awakening - Reflecting (15 minutes)

Have a volunteer read Matthew 25:34-46 (Page 1054). After silent reflection, read verses 35 and 36 again slowly. As each act of kindness is read, ask the participants to list the things they have done either as an individual or as a member of a group in the recent past that would be an appropriate response to these challenges in Scripture. When finished, share your list with each other. Then discuss the answers to the following questions: Why is it significant that this list of actions appears under the sub-heading of "The Judgment of the Nations?" In this context, how is kindness to others more than "just the nice thing to do?" Is extending kindness hard to do? Do you think society understands the importance of acts of kindness?

Group Prayer (5 minutes)

Leader: Father, reveal Your kindness to us through each other and everyone we meet. Accept these prayers, praises and petitions in spirit of kindness and love: **enter aloud all individual intentions.** We ask this through Your Son, our Lord Jesus Christ, Amen.

Closing Prayer (5 minutes)

Read the **Profile in Faith** article on Blessed Mother Teresa on insert page M-3. At the end, pause for a few moments in silent prayer.

Fellowship (15 minutes)

After the session is completed and while refreshments are served, play softly in the background: "The Lord is Kind and Merciful" from the Faith-Filled Catholic Women's Bible Music CD.

The Faith-Filled Catholic Women's Bible Study Program

Participant's Worksheet

Kindness   Insert M-1 through M-4

You can prepare for the discussion about the theme **Kindness** by thinking about how you would answer the following questions: What does the word "kindness" mean to me? What was a memorable time when someone showed me kindness? What did they do? How did I feel? How do I think society would be changed if more people treated others with kindness?

Read Luke 10:29-37 (Page 1112).

Why is it significant that the first two people who ignored the man in need were a Priest and a Levite?

What is symbolic about the fact that it was a Samaritan (someone from outside the mainstream of society) who extended kindness to the man in need?

What is a contemporary equivalent to this parable?

Why do I think we often react just as the Priest and Levite did to people in need?

Why is just "helping a little" not enough?

Read Matthew 25:34-46 (Page 1054).

What are some examples in my recent experience of how I responded in kindness by: Feeding the hungry; Giving drink to the thirsty; Welcoming a stranger; Clothing the naked; Visiting the imprisoned?

Why is it significant that this list of actions appears under the sub-heading of "The Judgment of the Nations?"

In this context, how is kindness to others more than "just the nice thing to do?"

Is extending kindness hard to do?

Do you think society understands the importance of acts of kindness?

Group Prayer - My intentions for group prayer this week:

My Personal Response in Kindness for this week - Extend kindness by sharing a special talent, a unique skill, or even your favorite recipe with another woman in your family or a close friend. In your sharing, tell them why you cherish it.

Other Scripture on **Kindness**:

Luke 6:35 (Page 1103) * 2 Corinthians 6:6 (Page 1259) * Galatians 5:22 (Page 1275)
Ephesians 4:32 (Page 1282) * Colossians 3:12-14 (Page 1296) * Hebrews 13:3 (Page 1338)

The Faith-Filled Catholic Women's Bible Study Program

A Leader's Guide for Group Discussion

Love	Insert N-1 through N-4
Song: "In Love We Choose to Live"	Composer: Jeanne Cotter
Disc 2, Track 3	Faith-Filled Catholic Women's Bible Music CD

Materials Needed

Faith-Filled Catholic Women's Bible and Music CD, CD player, Participant's Worksheet, Pad of Paper, Pen.

Setting the Stage

Before this session, send any member of the group that may not have been present at the last session the Participant's Worksheet for this session. Also, send a reminder of the date and time of the session as well as directions to the meeting place (if different from the church). To enhance an atmosphere of **Love**, have the song "In Love We Choose to Live" from the Faith-Filled Catholic Women's Bible Music CD playing in the background when the participants arrive.

Warm Up - Optional (10 minutes)

Moving around the group, have the first person say out loud the name of a person, place or thing in (or a word) associated with the Bible. The next person then must choose a new name of a person, place or thing or a word associated with the Bible **that begins with the last letter of the word the person before her said**. If a participant cannot think an answer, she must pass and is out of the game. The last person to answer is the winner. (Example: 1st person God 2nd person Daniel 3rd person Levite etc.)

Opening Discussion (10 minutes)

Have each participant share her answers to the following questions: Do you think love is a noun or a verb? Explain. Do you think of love as a feeling or as an action? Explain. Read 1 John 4:8 "Whoever is without love does not know God, for God is love." What does this verse mean to you?

Plan and Purpose (10 minutes)

Read together the **Plan and Purpose** article on insert page N-1. Then have each participant write down five actions in her life that she would consider love in action. Have each participant share and explain her list with the group. Discuss how love for others manifests itself in many ways.

Spiritual Awakening - Opening Prayer

Pray together the **Opening Prayer** at the top of insert page N-2.

Spiritual Awakening - Recognizing (10 minutes)

Ask for volunteers to read aloud each of the Scripture passages in the **Recognizing** section of **Spiritual Awakening** on insert page N-2. Remind the participants that each reader will pause for a few seconds of silence after each passage to allow anyone to offer any spontaneous thought, prayer, praise or thanksgiving that this Scripture might inspire. After the final Scripture is read, ask the group, "What else do these Scriptures teach us about **Love**?" Share and discuss any responses.

Spiritual Awakening Recognizing (10 minutes)

<u>**Leader:** Matthew 5:44 (Page 1016) challenges us to love our enemies and to pray for those who persecute us. What are the implications of this command in Scripture for: our homes, our communities, our country and our world? Is it really possible to "love your enemies?"</u> Discuss as a group. To conclude, ask each participant to share who they think is living this commandment. This can be someone famous or someone they know or have known.

Spiritual Awakening - Reflecting (10 minutes)

<u>Mother Teresa once said, "It is not how much we do, but how much love we put into doing. It is not how much we give, but the love we put in the giving."</u> Ask the participants to share with the group how giving sometimes can be done "not in a spirit of love?" Respond as a group to this question: What is your secret to performing your daily responsibilities (i.e. putting in a full day at work, preparing meals at home, shopping, cleaning the house, doing the laundry) in the spirit of love?

Group Prayer (5 minutes)

<u>**Leader:** Dearest Jesus, in Your passion, crucifixion and death, You revealed to us the ultimate meaning of love. Inspire us to imitate You in sacrifices of love for those close to us. We present our praises, prayers and petitions today in recognition of Your profound love for us: **enter aloud all individual intentions**. We pray that, out of Your infinite mercy and love for us, You will hear and answer our prayers. Amen.</u>

Closing Prayer (10 minutes)

Read 1 Corinthians 13:4-7 (Page 1244) slowly, pausing after each line to say,
"Holy Spirit, help us love as the Father has loved us."

Fellowship (15 minutes)

After the session is completed and while refreshments are served, play softly in the background: "In Love We Choose to Live" from the Faith-Filled Catholic Women's Bible Music CD.

The Faith-Filled Catholic Women's Bible Study Program

Participant's Worksheet

You can prepare for the discussion about the theme **Love** by thinking about how you would answer the following questions:

1. Do I think love is a feeling or an action? Explain.

2. What does "God is love" mean to me?

3. What are five things that I do in my everyday life that I would consider "love in action?"

4. How does love for others manifest itself in my life?

5. What are the implications of God's command to love my enemies at home, in town, in our country, in the world?

6. Is it really possible for me to love my enemies?

7. Who is someone (either famous or someone I know or have known) I think is living (or has lived) this commandment?

8. How can giving sometimes be done "not in a spirit of love?"

9. What is my secret to performing daily responsibilities in the spirit of love?

Group Prayer - My intentions for group prayer this week:

My Personal Response in Love for this week - During this week, mail or leave a special note to a family member reminding them how much you love them.

Other Scripture on **Love**:

Deuteronomy 7:9, 12-13 (Page 168) * Psalm 146:8 (Page 631) * Proverbs 8:17 (Page 640)
John 3:16 (Page 1141) * John 16:27 (Page 1161) * Romans 12:9-10 (Page 1223)
James 2:8 (Page 1343) * Ephesians 2:4 (Page 1279)
1 Thessalonians 4:9 (Page 1300) * 1 Peter 1:22 (Page 1349)
1 John 2:10 (Page 1360) * 1 John 4:9-21 (Page 1363)

The Faith-Filled Catholic Women's Bible Study Program

A Leader's Guide for Group Discussion

Loyalty   Insert O-1 through O-4
Song: "Sanctum nomen"   Composer: Margaret Rizza
Disc 2, Track 4   Faith-Filled Catholic Women's Bible Music CD

Materials Needed

Faith-Filled Catholic Women's Bible and Music CD, CD player, Participant's Worksheet, Index Card (each).

Setting the Stage

Before this session, send any member of the group that may not have been present at the last session the Participant's Worksheet for this session. Also, send a reminder of the date and time of the session as well as directions to the meeting place (if different from the church). To enhance an atmosphere of **Loyalty**, have the song "Sanctum nomen" from the Faith-Filled Catholic Women's Bible Music CD playing in the background when the participants arrive.

Warm Up - Optional (15 minutes)

Many people in the Bible lived lives (or made critical decisions in their life) that demonstrated loyalty in faith. Give each participant in the group an index card with one of the following 10 names on the card. Her challenge is to introduce herself to the rest of the group by answering only their yes or no questions designed to determine who she is. If a questioner gets a "no" answer, the next person in the group gets to ask a question. After each "yes" answer, the woman who asked the question gets **ONE** chance to guess the identity of the subject. Continue until each woman has had an opportunity to be the mystery Biblical guest or as long as time permits. Example of questions: (If the Subject was Ruth) Q. Did you live in the New Testament times? A. No (next questioner) Q. Are you a man? A. No. (next questioner) Were you loyal to another family member? A. Yes (same questioner gets to guess) Are you Sarah? A. No (next questioner) Do you have a Book of the Bible named after you? A. Yes (same questioner gets to guess) Are you Ruth? A. Yes. Choose from these characters: The Blessed Virgin Mary, Simeon, Ruth, Mary Magdalene, Father of Prodigal Son, Esther, the Apostle John, Joseph of Arimathea, Job, Anna.

Opening Discussion (10 minutes)

Ask each participant to share her answers to the following questions: When you hear the word loyalty, what do you think of? Relate a story from your experience that best illustrates loyalty. How can loyalty be misplaced, or even misunderstood in relationships?

Plan and Purpose (15 minutes)

Read as a group the **Plan and Purpose** article on insert page O-1. Then discuss these questions: What is (or was) the nature of the relationship between you and your husband's mother? How is it different from the relationship he has with your mother? After the discussion read aloud together Chapter 1 of the Book of Ruth (Page 238). Discuss what lessons this Scripture holds for us.

Spiritual Awakening - Opening Prayer

Pray together the **Opening Prayer** at the top of insert page O-2.

Spiritual Awakening - Recognizing (10 minutes)

Ask for volunteers to read aloud each of the Scripture passages in the **Recognizing** section of **Spiritual Awakening** on insert page O-2. Remind the participants that each reader will pause for a few seconds of silence after each passage to allow anyone to offer any spontaneous thought, prayer, praise or thanksgiving that this Scripture might inspire. After the final Scripture is read, ask the group, "What else do these Scriptures teach us about **Loyalty**?" Share and discuss any responses.

Spiritual Awakening - Reflecting (15 minutes)

Read Hebrews 13:5-8 (Page 1339). Discuss your answers to these questions with the group: What is your relationship with wealth and possessions? What are some examples in our society where loyalty is misplaced? Why is remaining loyal to God (being receptive to His will) sometimes difficult? How has God demonstrated His loyalty to you as promised in His words, "I will never forsake you or abandon you?"

Group Prayer (5 minutes)

Leader: Heavenly Father, in Your constant love and devotion, You have never forsaken or abandoned us. Lead us to strive for that same loyalty to You and to those we love. We ask You today to hear our praises, prayers and petitions: **enter aloud all individual intentions.** With loyal and humble hearts, in Jesus' name, Amen.

Closing Prayer (5 minutes)

Read the **Profile in Faith** article on Mary Magdalene on insert page O-3. Close with this prayer:

Oh God, help us to imitate the loyalty of Ruth in all our relationships with others and the loyalty of Mary Magdalene in our relationship with Your Son. Amen.

Fellowship (15 minutes)

After the session is completed and while refreshments are served, play softly in the background: "Sanctum nomen" from the Faith-Filled Catholic Women's Bible Music CD.

The Faith-Filled Catholic Women's Bible Study Program
Participant's Worksheet

<u>Loyalty</u>   Insert O-1 through O-4

You can prepare for the discussion about the theme **Loyalty** by thinking about how you would answer the following questions:

1. When I hear the word loyalty, what do I think of?

2. Relate a story from my experience that best illustrates loyalty.

3. How can loyalty be misplaced, or even misunderstood in relationships?

4. What is (or was) my relationship with my husband's mother? How is that relationship different from his relationship with my mother?

Read Hebrews 13:5-8 (Page 1339). What is my relationship with wealth and possessions?

What are some examples in our society where loyalty is misplaced?

Why is remaining loyal to God (being receptive to His will) sometimes difficult?

How has God demonstrated His loyalty to me as promised in His words "I will never forsake you or abandon you?"

Group Prayer - My intentions for group prayer this week:

My Personal Response in Loyalty for this week - Be diligent about honoring your commitments to someone in your role as a mother, wife, grandmother or friend. Begin by focusing on one area that you know needs attention in your life.

Closing Prayer -

O God, help us to imitate the loyalty of Ruth in all our relationships with others and the loyalty of Mary Magdalene in our relationship with Your Son, Amen.

Other Scripture on **Loyalty** (Faithfulness):

Matthew 7:24 (Page 1019) * Deuteronomy 31:6 (Page 190) * Psalm 89:2 (Page 599)
Psalm 119:90 (Page 619) * Isaiah 40:8 (Page 779) * Isaiah 41:10 (Page 780)
Romans 3:3 (Page 1213) * 1 Thessalonians 5:24 (Page 1301) * 2 Timothy 2:13 (Page 1315)

The Faith-Filled Catholic Women's Bible Study Program

A Leader's Guide for Group Discussion

Patience
Song: "Peace, Be Not Anxious"
Disc 2, Track 5

Insert P-1 through P-4
Composer: Lorie True
Faith-Filled Catholic Women's Bible Music CD

Materials Needed

Faith-Filled Catholic Women's Bible and Music CD, CD player, Participant's Worksheet, Candles.

Setting the Stage

Before this session, send any member of the group that may not have been present at the last session the Participant's Worksheet for this session. Also, send a reminder of the date and time of the session as well as directions to the meeting place (if different from the church). To enhance an atmosphere of **Patience**, have the song "Peace, Be Not Anxious" from the Faith-Filled Catholic Women's Bible Music CD playing in the background when the participants arrive.

Warm Up - Optional (10 minutes)

Ask the participants to use the back of their Participant's Worksheet to answer the questions about how much patience they exhibit in these life situations.

1. The driver of the car at the light in front of you doesn't move because they do not see that the light has turned green. What do you do?
2. When you get to the minor emergency center with an injury to yourself or family member; you find your are 14th in line. What do you do?
3. Your spouse or a family member is taking forever to get ready to go out. You have been ready for 30 minutes and are already 15 minutes late. He or she is still not ready. What do you do?
4. Have any of your family or friends told you that you need to slow down?
5. You find yourself on a committee with two newcomers who have a lot of radical ideas about how to do a job you have been familiar with for years. How would you approach the situation?
6. Someone is telling you a story and taking forever to get to the point. What do you do?
7. Your waiter (in a nearly empty restaurant) is laughing and joking with her friend at the bar 20 minutes after she took your order. What would you do?
8. When you put something in the microwave for 2 minutes. How do you pass the time?
9. What do you usually do with your hands while you are talking on the phone?
10. An item you are wanting will not be in the store for 10 days. However, you can order it on-line and have it in 3 days if you pay extra. Which do you do?
When completed, have some fun sharing your answers with each other.

Opening Discussion (10 minutes)

Leader: Ask the participants to share their answers to these two questions: What little inconveniences in life try your patience (traffic, lines, etc.)? What secrets do you have to keeping your patience when it is tested? After the discussion, read together the **Plan and Purpose** article on insert page P-1.

Spiritual Awakening - Opening Prayer

Pray together the **Opening Prayer** at the top of insert page P-2.

Spiritual Awakening Recognizing (10 minutes)

Ask for volunteers to read aloud each of the Scripture passages in the **Recognizing** section of **Spiritual Awakening** on insert page P-2. Remind the participants that each reader will pause for a few seconds of silence after each passage to allow anyone to offer any spontaneous thought, prayer, praise or thanksgiving that this Scripture might inspire. After the final Scripture is read, discuss as a group individual answers to these questions: Do you think God has patience with you? When and how is God's patience most evident?

Spiritual Awakening - Reflecting (15 minutes)

Read Matthew 18:21-35 (Page 1039). Have the participants discuss their answers to these questions: Are you indebted to someone who is waiting on you for something? How patient are you with anyone who may be in debt to you (even if only emotionally)? How patient are you in waiting for repayment of a favor? How patient are you in waiting for the fulfillment of a promise made? How patient are you in waiting for an apology after a disagreement? Share some instances where your patience was tried and rewarded?

Spiritual Awakening - Reflecting (15 minutes)

Read Matthew 7:7-8 (Page 1018). Remind the participants that God assures us in this Scripture that our prayers will be answered. Have any volunteers share with the group an instance in their life when God's answer to their prayer was not what they expected or did not happen when they hoped it would.

Group Prayer/ Closing Prayer - (15 minutes)

Read the **Faith In Action** article "Wait and Pray" on insert page P-2. After a moment of silence together, say the following prayer: <u>**Leader:** Heavenly Father, in full confidence that You answer all our prayers, we come forward today to light a candle as a symbol of our faith in You. May the light of your love burn in our hearts as we offer up our intentions to You today</u> . . .

(Each woman comes forward to light a candle after which she **enters aloud her individual intentions.** After the last participant has lit her candle, all pray together: **. . . give us a patient heart to wait for the answers to our prayers according to the schedule You choose. Give us the ability and willingness to recognize the answers You send. May the light of Christ shine in our lives. Amen.**

Fellowship (15 minutes)

After the session is completed and while refreshments are served, play softly in the background: "Peace, Be Not Anxious" from the Faith-Filled Catholic Women's Bible Music CD.

The Faith-Filled Catholic Women's Bible Study Program

Participant's Worksheet

Patience   Insert P-1 through P-4

You can prepare for the discussion about the theme **Patience** by thinking about how you would answer the following questions:

1. What little inconveniences in life try my patience (traffic, lines, etc.)?

2. What secrets do I have to keeping my patience when it is tried?

3. Do I think God has patience with me? When and how is God's patience most evident?

4. Am I indebted to someone who is waiting on me for something?

5. How patient am I with anyone who may be in debt to me (even if only emotionally)?

6. How patient am I in waiting for repayment of a favor?

7. How patient am I in waiting for the fulfillment of a promise?

8. How patient am I in waiting for or an apology after a disagreement?

9. What are some instances where my patience was tried and rewarded?

10. What is one instance in my life when God's answer to my prayer was not what I expected or did not happen when I hoped it would?

Group Prayer - My intentions for group prayer this week:

Closing Prayer -

Leader: Heavenly Father, in full confidence that You answer all our prayers, we come forward today to light a candle as a symbol of our faith in You. May the light of Your love burn in our hearts as we offer up our intentions to You today . . . Each woman comes forward to light a candle after which she **enters aloud her individual intentions**. After the last participant has lit her candle, all pray together:

Give us a patient heart to wait for the answers to our prayers according to the schedule You choose and the ability and willingness to recognize the answers You send. May the light of Christ shine in our lives. Amen.

My Personal Response in Patience for this week - Remove one temptation to sin that you know God has been patiently waiting for you to remove from your life. Pray for the strength to keep it away every day.

Other Scripture on **Patience**:
Ecclesiastes 3:1 (Page 666) * Galatians 5:22 (Page 1275)
1 Thessalonians 5:14 (Page 1301) * 1 Timothy 6:11 (Page 1311)
Hebrews 6:12 (Page 1329)

The Faith-Filled Catholic Women's Bible Study Program

A Leader's Guide for Group Discussion

Peace
Song: "Calm Me, Lord"
Disc 2, Track 6

Insert Q-1 through Q-4
Composer: Margaret Rizza
Faith-Filled Catholic Women's Bible Music CD

Materials Needed

Faith-Filled Catholic Women's Bible and Music CD, CD player, Incense, Participant's Worksheet.

Setting the Stage

Before this session, send any member of the group that may not have been present at the last session the Participant's Worksheet for this session. Also, send a reminder of the date and time of the session as well as directions to the meeting place (if different from the church). To enhance an atmosphere of **Peace**, have the song "Calm Me, Lord" from the Faith-Filled Catholic Women's Bible Music CD playing in the background when the participants arrive.

Warm Up - Optional (10 Minutes)

To create an atmosphere of quiet, calm and peace, ask the participants to begin by sitting relaxed with their eyes closed for a couple minutes of silence. Lowering the lights and/or burning incense in the room will help to create the most effective mood. After a few minutes of silence, ask the participants to keep their eyes closed as **you softly say this prayer**:

**Calm me, Lord, as you calmed the storm;
still me, Lord, keep me from harm.
Let all the tumult within me cease,
enfold me, Lord, in your peace.**

Then, ask the participants to open their eyes and pray together, the same prayer again (found at the top of the Participant's Worksheet). Immediately following the prayer, ask the participants to relax as you listen to "Calm Me, Lord" Disc 2, Track 6 of the Faith-Filled Catholic Women's Bible Music CD.

Opening Discussion (15 minutes)

Moving around the group, have each participant share her answers to the following questions:

What is peace? Have you ever felt truly at peace? What is the opposite of peace in your life? What causes you to worry and have anxiety?

Spiritual Awakening - Opening Prayer

Pray together the **Opening Prayer** at the top of insert page Q-2.

Spiritual Awakening - Recognizing (10 minutes)

Ask for volunteers to read aloud each of the Scripture passages in the **Recognizing** section of **Spiritual Awakening** on insert page Q-2. Remind the participants that each reader will pause for a few seconds of silence after each passage to allow anyone to offer any spontaneous thought, prayer, praise or thanksgiving that this Scripture might inspire.

Spiritual Awakening - Reflecting (15 minutes)

Read Philippians 4:4-9 (Page 1291). Ask the participants to share a recent time when they were worried or anxious and struggled to turn a concern over to God. Did they ultimately find peace? If so, how?

Faith In Action (20 minutes)

Read the **Faith in Action** article "Winning at Practice" on insert page Q-4. Then, discuss as a group the following questions: What is it that makes life sometimes seem like a series of races that must be won? What do you do to minimize stress and pressure in your life? Share with the group your experience with someone you know who seems at peace. Why do you think they feel that way?

Group Prayer

Leader: We offer our prayers, praises and petitions this week especially asking for Your blessing of peace in our lives: **enter aloud all individual intentions.** Heavenly Father, in Your infinite mercy, give us peace in our lives, peace in our families and peace in the world. We ask this in Jesus name. Amen.

Closing Prayer (5 minutes)

Close by saying together the Prayer of St. Francis:

Lord, make me an instrument of Your peace.
Where there is hatred, let me sow love; where there is injury, pardon;
where there is doubt, faith; where there is despair, hope;
where there is darkness, light; and where there is sadness, joy.
O, Divine Master, grant that I may not so much seek to be consoled as to console;
to be understood as to understand; to be loved as to love;
for it is in giving that we receive; it is in pardoning that we are pardoned;
and it is in dying that we are born to eternal life. Amen.

Fellowship (15 minutes)

After the session is completed and while refreshments are served, play softly in the background: "Calm Me, Lord" from the Faith-Filled Catholic Women's Bible Music CD.

The Faith-Filled Catholic Women's Bible Study Program

Participant's Worksheet

Peace _____ Insert Q-1 through Q-4

Prayer for use during the Warm Up:

**Calm me, Lord, as you calmed the storm; still me, Lord, keep me from harm.
Let all the tumult within me cease, enfold me, Lord, in your peace.**

You can prepare for the discussion about the theme **Peace** by thinking about how you would answer the following questions:

1. What is peace? Have I ever felt truly at peace? What is the opposite of peace in my life?

2. What causes me to worry and have anxiety?

3. When was a time that I was worried or anxious and struggled to turn a concern over to God?

4. Did I ultimately find peace? If so, how?

5. What is it that makes life sometimes seem like a series of races that must be won?

6. What do I do to minimize stress and pressure in my life?

7. Who is someone I know who seems at peace. Why do I think they feel that way?

Group Prayer - My intentions for group prayer this week:

Closing Prayer -
Lord, make me an instrument of Your peace.
Where there is hatred, let me sow love; where there is injury, pardon;
where there is doubt, faith; where there is despair, hope;
where there is darkness, light; and where there is sadness, joy.
O, Divine Master, grant that I may not so much seek to be consoled as to console;
to be understood as to understand; to be loved as to love;
for it is in giving that we receive; it is in pardoning that we are pardoned;
and it is in dying that we are born to eternal life. Amen.

My Personal Response in Peace for this week - Focus on a tendency that you struggle with in regard to maintaining peace in your relationships (being sarcastic, talking down to others, being dismissive of others ideas, being abrasive, etc.). Memorize Romans 12:18 (Page 1224) and remind yourself to pray this verse when you are tempted to respond in a sinful way.

Other Scripture on **Peace**:

Psalm 85:9 (Page 598) * Psalm 122:7 (Page 622) * Isaiah 57:19 (Page 795)

Luke 2:14 (Page 1095) * Luke 10:5-6 (Page 1111) * John 16:33 (Page 1161)

Ephesians 2:14-18 (Page 1279) *

2 Thessalonians 3:16 (Page 1305)

The Faith-Filled Catholic Women's Bible Study Program

A Leader's Guide for Group Discussion

Sacrifice	Insert R-1 through R-4
Song: "Shadows Gather, Deep and Cold"	Composer: Kathy Powell
Disc 2, Track 7	Faith-Filled Catholic Women's Bible Music CD

Materials Needed

Faith-Filled Catholic Women's Bible and Music CD, CD player, Participant's Worksheet, Copies of the First Eucharistic Prayer (1 each), One copy of the Catechism of the Catholic Church.

Setting the Stage

Before this session, send any member of the group that may not have been present at the last session the Participant's Worksheet for this session. Also, send a reminder of the date and time of the session as well as directions to the meeting place (if different from the church). To enhance an atmosphere of **Sacrifice**, have the song "Shadows Gather, Deep and Cold" from the Faith-Filled Catholic Women's Bible Music CD playing in the background when the participants arrive.

Warm Up - Optional (15 Minutes)

Have each participant write the numbers 1 through (?) (however many participants there are in the group) down the left side of the back of the Participant's Worksheet. Below this list, jot down one sacrifice you have made at some time in your life and one sacrifice that YOU DID NOT MAKE. After everyone is finished, ask the first person to read the two sacrifices she wrote down. Identify them as A. and B. The challenge for everyone else is to identify (by listing it behind the appropriate number for each person) the sacrifice that is false from each participant's list of two sacrifices. For instance if I believe person # 3's second sacrifice is false (or did not happen) then my answer for #3 on the back of my Participant's Worksheet would be "B." Some examples of sacrifices could include: a) I quit a full time job and stayed home for 2 years when my daughter was born. b) I took a second job working three nights a week for 6 months when my husband changed jobs. c) I often did the cooking at home when I was a teenager to help my mother out. d) I cancelled my membership to the gym in order accommodate a friend's schedule so we could workout together. e) I did my mother-in-law's taxes for her after my husband's father died and refused to accept any payment. (etc.) Encourage the participants to be creative enough to make the "false" sacrifice very believable. The challenge is for each participant to fool the others. Compare your scores after the test when each individual identifies the sacrifice that they made up.

Opening Discussion (15 minutes)

Have the participants discuss the following questions: What do you remember about the role of sacrifice in the Old Testament? Why were sacrifices so important to the Hebrew people? After brief discussion, read the **Plan and Purpose** article on insert page R-1. Then, have each participant share her answers to the following questions: What sacrifices do you make routinely in life? Who do you think these sacrifices are for? Do you often think about everyday sacrifices you make in the context of your faith?

Spiritual Awakening - Opening Prayer

Pray together the **Opening Prayer** at the top of insert page R-2.

Spiritual Awakening - Recognizing (10 minutes)

Ask for volunteers to read aloud each of the passages in the **Recognizing** section of **Spiritual Awakening** on insert page R-2. Remind the participants that each reader will pause for a few seconds of silence after each passage to allow anyone to offer any spontaneous thought, prayer, praise or thanksgiving that this Scripture might inspire.

Spiritual Awakening - Reflecting (15 minutes)

Read Genesis 22:1-19 (Page 26). Then, ask the participants to share their answers to these questions: How important is sacrificing in defining your relationship with God? If you made a list of things most important in your life, where would God fall on that list? Why is it so difficult sometimes to answer God's call to have faith in the circumstances in our lives?

Spiritual Awakening - Reflecting (15 minutes)

Prayerfully read the First Eucharistic Prayer. Pause after each line and/or paragraph to discuss what you think the words mean. Then, read this paragraph 1419 from the Catechism of the Catholic Church:

Having passed from this world to the Father, Christ gives us in the Eucharist the pledge of glory with him. Participation in the Holy Sacrifice identifies us with his Heart, sustains our strength along the pilgrimage of this life, makes us long for eternal life, and unites us even now to the Church in heaven, the Blessed Virgin Mary, and all the saints.

Ask: How are you united with Christ's perfect sacrifice at Mass? How does attending Mass affect your life?

Group Prayer

Leader: Dearest Jesus, accept our prayers, praises and petitions this week with our deepest appreciation for the sacrifice You offered to the Father on our behalf: **enter aloud all individual intentions.** Inspire us to participate fully in Your sacrifice not only in our worship, but in how we live our daily lives. Amen.

Closing Prayer (5 minutes)

Have each participant complete this sentence (silently if preferred) with some cross they are currently bearing.

O Jesus, I embrace the cross of _____.
Because you carried your cross for me, I carry this cross for you.

Fellowship (15 minutes)

After the session is completed and while refreshments are served, play softly in the background: "Shadows Gather, Deep and Cold" from the Faith-Filled Catholic Women's Bible Music CD.

The Faith-Filled Catholic Women's Bible Study Program

Participant's Worksheet

Sacrifice   Insert R-1 through R-4

You can prepare for the discussion about the theme **Sacrifice** by thinking about how you would answer the following questions:

1. What do I remember about the role of sacrifice in the Old Testament?

2. Why were sacrifices so important to the Hebrew people?

3. What sacrifices do I make routinely in life? Who do I think these sacrifices are for?

4. Do I often think about the everyday sacrifices I make in the context of my faith?

Read Genesis 22:1-19 (Page 26) - How important is sacrificing in defining your relationship with God?

If I made a list of things most important in my life, where would God fall on that list?

Why is it so difficult sometimes to answer God's call to have faith in the circumstances in my life?

Read paragraph 1419 from the Catechism of the Catholic Church - Then answer:

How am I united with Christ's perfect sacrifice at Mass?

How does attending Mass affect my life?

Group Prayer - My intentions for group prayer this week:

Closing Prayer -

> **O Jesus, I embrace the cross of _____.**
> **Because you carried your cross for me, I carry this cross for you.**

My Personal Response in Sacrifice for this week - Just as Abram responded to the blessings of the priest Malchizedek in Genesis 14:20 (Page 20) re-evaluate how you are responding to God's blessings in your life. Is your time, talent and treasure being given in a true spirit of sacrificial giving?

Other Scripture on **Sacrifice**:

Matthew 26:28 (Page 1056) * Ephesians 5:2 (Page 1282)

Philippians 2:17 (Page 1289) Philippians 4:18 (Page 1291) Hebrews 10:1-18 (Page 1334)

Hebrews 11:4 (Page 1336) * Hebrews 13:15 (Page 1339)

The Faith-Filled Catholic Women's Bible Study Program

A Leader's Guide for Group Discussion

Suffering   Insert S-1 through S-4
Song: "If Jesus Wept"   Composer: Carol Browning
Disc 2, Track 8   Faith-Filled Catholic Women's Bible Music CD

Materials Needed

Faith-Filled Catholic Women's Bible and Music CD, CD player, Participant's Worksheet, Words to the Prayer of Abandonment (on Participant's Worksheet).

Setting the Stage

Before this session, send any member of the group that may not have been present at the last session the Participant's Worksheet for this session. Also, send a reminder of the date and time of the session as well as directions to the meeting place (if different from the church). To enhance an atmosphere of **Suffering**, have the song "If Jesus Wept" from the Faith-Filled Catholic Women's Bible Music CD playing in the background when the participants arrive.

Warm Up Optional (10 minutes)

Have the participants take a few minutes to write their answer to this question on the back of their copy of the Participant s Worksheet:

If you had the power to eliminate one kind of suffering in the world, what would it be? Share and discuss your answers.

Opening Discussion (20 minutes)

Read the **Plan and Purpose** article on insert page S-1. Then discuss the following questions: Why do you think bad things happen to good people? How does Jesus show us how to respond to suffering in our lives? Pope John Paul II often spoke of the salvific power of suffering. What does that mean to you?

Spiritual Awakening - Opening Prayer

Pray together the **Opening Prayer** at the top of insert page S-2.

Spiritual Awakening Recognizing (15 minutes)

Ask for volunteers to read aloud each of the Scripture passages in the **Recognizing** section of **Spiritual Awakening** on insert page S-2. Remind the participants that each reader will pause for a few seconds of silence after each passage to allow anyone to offer any spontaneous thought, prayer, praise or thanksgiving that this Scripture might inspire.

Spiritual Awakening - Reflecting (20 minutes)

Read 1 Peter 1:6-7 (Page 1348). Then, ask the group to share their answers to these questions: Has there been one area of your life where you feel God has (or is) testing you through some hardship? Do you think that you have passed (or are passing) the test? How has your own suffering changed the way you look at the trials of others?

Faith in Action - (20 minutes)

Read the **Faith in Action** article "The Art of Dying" on insert page S-4. Discuss answers to the following questions: Is there someone you admire because of the way they handle suffering in their life? Share an experience about how someone close to you handled suffering during a terminal illness. What role does your faith play in helping you endure suffering in life?

Group Prayer

Leader: Heavenly Father, give us the courage to accept suffering in our life not as a burden but as an opportunity to share with You. Hear and answer these special prayers, praises and petitions as our group prayer for all those who endure suffering each day: **enter aloud all individual intentions.** We ask You this, in Jesus' name. Amen.

Closing Prayer (5 minutes)

As a group, pray the "Prayer of Abandonment" by Charles Foucauld.

**Father, I abandon myself into your hands; do with me what you will.
Whatever you may do, I thank you: I am ready for all, I accept all.
Let only your will be done in me, and in all your creatures
I wish no more than this, O Lord. Into your hands I commend my soul;
I offer it to you with all the love of my heart, for I love you Lord,
and so need to give myself, to surrender myself into your hands,
without reserve, and with boundless confidence, for you are my Father.**

Fellowship (15 minutes)

After the session is completed and while refreshments are served, play softly in the background: "Shadows Gather, Deep and Cold" from the Fireside Women's Bible CD or other appropriate music.

The Faith-Filled Catholic Women's Bible Study Program

Participant's Worksheet

Suffering   Insert S-1 through S-4
_____

You can prepare for the discussion about the theme **Suffering** by thinking about how you would answer the following questions:

1. Why do I think bad things happen to good people?

2. How does Jesus show me how to respond to suffering in my life?

3. Pope John Paul II often spoke of the salvific power of suffering. What does that mean to me?

Read 1 Peter 1:6-7 (Page 1348).
Has there been one area of my life where I feel God has (or is) testing me through some hardship?

Do I think that I have passed (or am passing) the test?

How has my own suffering changed the way I look at the trials of others?

Read the **Faith in Action** article "The Art of Dying" on insert page S-4.

Who do I admire because of the way they handle suffering in their life?

My experience with how someone close to me handled suffering during a terminal illness. What role does my faith play in helping me endure suffering in life?

Group Prayer - My intentions for group prayer this week:

Closing Prayer -   **The Prayer of Abandonment**
                                          by Charles de Foucauld
**Father, I abandon myself into your hands; do with me what you will.
Whatever you may do, I thank you: I am ready for all, I accept all.
Let only your will be done in me, and in all your creatures
I wish no more than this, O Lord. Into your hands I commend my soul;
I offer it to you with all the love of my heart, for I love you Lord,
and so need to give myself, to surrender myself into your hands,
without reserve, and with boundless confidence, for you are my Father.**

My Personal Response in Suffering for this week - Talk to your children or grandchildren about how they react to suffering. Encourage them to see how God uses suffering to draw us closer to Him.

Other Scripture on **Suffering**:

Deuteronomy 8:2-3 (Page 169) * Matthew 10:38 (Page 1024)
Romans 8:35-39 (Page 1219) * 2 Corinthians 1:3-11 (Page 1252)
1 Peter 2:21 (Page 1350) * Philippians 3:10-11 (Page 1290)
Hebrews 12:4-11 (Page 1337) * 2 Corinthians 4:7-12 (Page 1256)

The Faith-Filled Catholic Women's Bible Study Program

A Leader's Guide for Group Discussion

Theme: Triumph
Song: "My Soul, Triumphant in the Lord"
Disc 2, Track 9

Insert: T-1 through T-4
Composer: Alice Parker
Faith-Filled Catholic Women's Bible Music CD

Materials Needed

Faith-Filled Catholic Women's Bible and Music CD, CD player, Participant's Worksheet, Crucifix, Incense.

Setting the Stage

Before this session, send any member of the group that may not have been present at the last session the Participant's Worksheet for this session. Also, send a reminder of the date and time of the session as well as directions to the meeting place (if different from the church). To enhance an atmosphere of **Triumph**, have the song "My Soul, Triumphant in the Lord" from the Faith-Filled Catholic Women's Bible Music CD playing in the background when the participants arrive.

Warm Up Optional (10 minutes)

Have the participants take a few minutes to think about their answers to the following questions: Other than Christ, who would you say accomplished the greatest feat or won the biggest triumph in human history? Who is someone you admire or look up to as a "winner?" These people can be from any generation, any walk of life or any discipline. Ask each participant to share her answers with the group and her reasons for choosing who she did.

Opening Discussion (15 minutes)

Ask the participants: Have you ever won a race? If so, what were the circumstances? Have you ever received a trophy or an award for something you did or participated in? If so, explain. Have you ever won a contest or something unexpectedly? Following this discussion, read the **Plan and Purpose** article on insert page T-1. Discuss the answers to the following questions: As a Christian, where does your triumph come from? How is our pursuit of triumph in Christ enhanced as Catholics?

Spiritual Awakening - Opening Prayer

Pray together the **Opening Prayer** at the top of insert page T-2.

Spiritual Awakening - Recognizing (5 minutes)

Ask for volunteers to read aloud each of the Scripture passages in the **Recognizing** section of **Spiritual Awakening** on insert page T-2. Remind the participants that each reader will pause for a few seconds of silence after each passage to allow anyone to offer any spontaneous thought, prayer, praise or thanksgiving that this Scripture might inspire.

Spiritual Awakening - Reflecting (15 minutes)

Read 1 Corinthians 15:50-58 (Page 1248). Then, ask the participants to share their answers to these questions: Why is this Scripture uplifting? What do you believe heaven is going to be like? If our bodies will be made whole in heaven, what will we look like there? How old will we be? What about our loved ones? Discuss in general the participant's visions of what heaven will be like.

Faith in Action - (20 minutes)

Read the **Faith in Action** article "Little Triumphs" on insert page T-4. Ask the participants to identify what they think are the little triumphs in their lives? Then ask them to consider this statement: **"If the final triumph of reaching heaven could be broken down into a series of "little triumphs" that must be gained along your journey of faith, what would some of these be for you?"** Have the group take 5 minutes for each participant to record her thoughts to this question on the back of the Participant's Worksheet. Ask the group to share their answers. Then, ask any participant to share a story from her experience about someone they knew who has used a positive attitude and a strong faith to overcome seemingly insurmountable obstacles in their life.

Group Prayer

Leader: Dearest Jesus, with hope in our hearts that we too will triumph over sin and death through an eternal reward in heaven, we humbly ask You to hear and answer these special prayers, praises and petitions: **enter aloud all individual intentions**. Give us the strength to triumph in faith through a life dedicated to You. Amen.

Closing Prayer (10 minutes)

Place a crucifix in a prominent place in the room. As a group, spend time in quiet contemplation before the crucifix focused on the triumph of the cross. Burn some incense and play the song, "Sanctum nomen" on Disc 1, Track 3 from the Faith-Filled Catholic Women's Bible Music CD softly in the background to create a prayerful atmosphere. Then, after a few minutes of silence once the song finishes, say together the following prayer:

Behold, O kind and gentle Jesus, I kneel before you and pray that you would impress upon my heart the virtues of faith, hope, and charity, with true repentance for my sins and a firm purpose of amendment. At the same time, with sorrow I meditate on your five precious wounds having in mind the words which David spoke in prophecy: 'They have pierced my hands and my feet, I can count all my bones.' (Psalm 22)

Fellowship (15 minutes)

After the session is completed and while refreshments are served, play softly in the background: "My Soul, Triumphant in the Lord" or "Sanctum nomen" from the Faith-Filled Catholic Women's Bible Music CD.

The Faith-Filled Catholic Women's Bible Study Program

Participant's Worksheet

<u>Triumph</u>   Insert T-1 through T-4

You can prepare for the discussion about the theme **Triumph** by thinking about how you would answer the following questions:

1. Have I ever won a race? If so, what were the circumstances?

2. Did I ever receive a trophy or an award for something I did or participated in?

3. Did I ever win a contest or something unexpectedly?

4. As a Christian, where does my triumph come from?

5. How is our pursuit of triumph in Christ enhanced as a Catholic?

Read 1 Corinthians 15:50-58 (Page 1248). Why is the Scripture uplifting?

What do I believe heaven is going to be like?

If our bodies will be made whole in heaven, what will I look like there? How old will I be? What about my loved ones?

Read the Faith in Action article "Little Triumphs" on insert page T-4.

What do I consider to be some of the little triumphs in my life?

If the final triumph of reaching heaven could be broken down into a series of "little triumphs" that must be gained along my journey of faith, what are some of these for me?

Who is someone I know whose faith and attitude helped them overcome seemingly insurmountable obstacles?

Group Prayer - My intentions for group prayer this week:

Closing Prayer -

Prayer Before the Crucifix
Behold, O kind and gentle Jesus, I kneel before you and pray that You would impress upon my heart the virtues of faith, hope, and charity, with true repentance for my sins and a firm purpose of amendment. At the same time, with sorrow I meditate on Your five precious wounds having in mind the words which David spoke in prophecy: "They have pierced my hands and my feet, I can count all my bones." (Psalm 22)

My Personal Response in Triumph for this week - Resolve to triumph over a bad habit or some sin in your life. Write down some specific things you will dedicate yourself to in this personal battle.

Other Scripture on **Triumph**:

Job 20:5 (Page 531) * John 14:2-3 (Page 1158) * Romans 6:8-11 (Page 1216)
Colossians 2:15 (Page 1295) * 2 Timothy 1:10 (Page 1314)

The Faith-Filled Catholic Women's Bible Study Program

A Leader's Guide for Group Discussion

Theme: Understanding
Song: "We Will Remember"
Disc 2, Track 10

Insert U-1 through U-4
Composer: Susan J. Paul
Faith-Filled Catholic Women's Bible Music CD

Materials Needed

Faith-Filled Catholic Women's Bible and Music CD, CD player, Participant's Worksheet, Seeds, Potting Soil, Small Pots.

Setting the Stage

Before this session, send any member of the group that may not have been present at the last session the Participant's Worksheet for this session. Also, send a reminder of the date and time of the session as well as directions to the meeting place (if different from the church). To enhance an atmosphere of **Understanding**, have the song "We Will Remember" from the Faith-Filled Catholic Women's Bible Music CD playing in the background when the participants arrive.

Warm Up - Optional (10 minutes)

The purpose of this exercise is to demonstrate how difficult understanding is and how often it breaks down in the process of communicating information from one person to another. The leader begins this exercise by whispering the sentence below into the ear of the person on her right. Instruct each participant to whisper exactly what she heard to the person on her right until the message gets to the very last person in the group. Have that person say out loud what she understood the exact message to be. Then have the leader read the original message. To demonstrate how difficult this is, make up a new shorter sentence and try it again.

**A brown dog chased a maroon car driven by a girl with long blond hair
as her boyfriend held three tomatoes in a sack on his lap.**

Discuss how and where the group thinks the message changed along the way.

Opening Discussion (15 minutes)

Ask each participant to share her answers to the following questions: What does it mean to truly understand something? How can you tell if someone doesn't understand you? Why do you think understanding is so important when it comes to reading the Bible? After the discussion, read the **Plan and Purpose** article on insert page U-1. Ask the participants: How is understanding related to peace and contentment in the context of faith?

Spiritual Awakening - Opening Prayer

Pray together the **Opening Prayer** at the top of insert page U-2.

Spiritual Awakening - Recognizing (5 minutes)

Ask a volunteer to prayerfully read each of the Scripture passages in the **Recognizing** section of **Spiritual Awakening** on insert page U-2. Remind the readers to pause after each verse for a few moments of silence to allow any participant to spontaneously share any special meaning that verse has for her.

Spiritual Awakening - Reflecting (15 minutes)

Read John 8:31-59 (Page 1150). Then, ask the group to share their answers to these questions: How did the Jews respond to Jesus? What does this same response look like in today's society? Do you ever catch yourself responding to a Catholic teaching in the same way? Read verses 42 and 43 again. Are there some teachings that we as a Church can't bear to hear? What about the phenomenon of being a cafeteria Catholic? Do we make this mistake in relation to some issues?

Faith in Action - (15 minutes)

Read the **Faith In Action** article on insert page U-4. Share your favorite story or any experience you have had where childhood innocence exposed a deeper understanding of some situation. Discuss answers to the following questions: How can having the understanding of a child help us to understand better God's purpose for our lives? Why do you believe Christ was so aware of the children around Him?

Group Prayer (5 minutes)

Leader: God, our Father, help us to understand Your plan and purpose for us in life. Help us to realize that imitating the example of Your Son will never be easy and that if we turn our back on Him by ignoring any part of His message, we are turning our back on You. We ask You to hear and answer our special prayers, praises and petitions today: **enter aloud all individual intentions**. Hear these prayers and to lead us to a fuller understanding of Your will as revealed in Scripture. In Jesus' name we pray, Amen.

Closing Prayer/Activity (10 minutes)

Read Matthew 13:18-23 (Page 1029), the explanation of the Parable of the Sower. As the song, "We Will Remember" plays softly in the background have each participant, in silence, plant seeds in a small pot with potting soil. Close by all reciting together a Glory Be.

Fellowship (15 minutes)

After the session is completed and while refreshments are served, play softly in the background: "We Will Remember" from the Faith-Filled Catholic Women's Bible Music CD.

The Faith-Filled Catholic Women's Bible Study Program

Participant's Worksheet

Understanding   Insert U-1 through U-4

You can prepare for the discussion about the theme **Understanding** by thinking about how you would answer the following questions:

1. What does it mean to truly understand something?

2. How can you tell if someone doesn't understand you?

3. Why do you think understanding is so important when it comes to reading the Bible?

4. How is understanding related to peace and contentment in the context of faith?

Read John 8:31-59 (Page 1150). How did the Jews respond to Jesus?

What does this same response look like in today's society?

Do you ever catch yourself responding to a Christian teaching in the same way?

Are there some teachings that we as a Church can't bear to hear? Give examples.

What about the phenomenon of being a cafeteria Catholic? Do I make this mistake in relation to some issues?

My favorite story or any experience I have had where childhood innocence exposed a deeper understanding of some situation.

How can having the understanding of a child help us to understand better God's purpose for our lives?

Why do I believe Christ was so aware of the children around Him?

Group Prayer - My intentions for group prayer this week:

My Personal Response in Understanding for this week - Reach out to someone in your life who is doing something you cannot understand. Make an attempt to see the situation from their perspective.

Other Scripture on **Understanding**:

Psalm 25:4 (Page 560) * Proverbs 3:5 (Page 636) * Proverbs 19:8 (Page 651)
Wisdom 7:17-21 (Page 686) * Ephesians 1:13-19 (Page 1278)

The Faith-Filled Catholic Women's Bible Study Program

A Leader's Guide for Group Discussion

Theme: Wisdom
Song: "Benediction"
Disc 2, Track 11

Insert V-1 through V-4
Composer: Carol Browning
Faith-Filled Catholic Women's Bible Music CD

Materials Needed

Faith-Filled Catholic Women's Bible and Music CD, CD player, Participant's Worksheet.

Setting the Stage

Before this session, send any member of the group that may not have been present at the last session the Participant's Worksheet for this session. Also, send a reminder of the date and time of the session as well as directions to the meeting place (if different from the church). To enhance an atmosphere of **Wisdom**, have the song "Benediction" from the Faith-Filled Catholic Women's Bible Music CD playing in the background when the participants arrive.

Warm Up - Optional (10 minutes)

Each of these 20 phrases is the first part of a well known saying, which could be from a movie, poem, speech, adage, or just about anything. Finish each statement on the back of your Participant's Worksheet. The Leader will read only the clues while the group will write only the answers.

Clues   Answer
1. If it's not broken....**don't fix it.**
2. It never rains....**it pours.**
3. Better late.... **than never**
4. It's not over until.... (problems 4 & 5 are interchangeable) . . . **it's over.**
5. It's not over until....**the fat lady sings.**
6. Whether you think that you can or that you can't....**you are usually right.**
7. The bigger they are....**the harder they fall.**
8. If it wasn't for bad luck....**I wouldn't have any luck at all.**
9. Never mix business....**with pleasure.**
10. Can't live with them....**can't live without them.**
11. Life is like a bowl....**of cherries.**
12. Go ahead, punk....**make my day.**
13. See no evil....**hear no evil.**
14. That which does not kill me....**only makes me stronger.**
15. To be or not to be....**that is the question.**
16. Four score and....**seven years ago.**
17. Don't count your chickens....**before they hatch.**
18. Jack and Jill went up the hill....**to fetch a pail of water.**
19. I think, therefore....**I am.**
20. Great spirits have always encountered violent opposition....**from mediocre minds.**

Test by William F. Bultas

Share your scores with each other.

Opening Discussion (15 minutes)

Ask these four quick questions In rapid succession. Have each of the participants write their answers to the following questions:

1. What is the first thing that comes to mind when you think of the word wisdom?

2. Name a person from history who you consider to be wise?

3. Who is the wisest person you know?

4. If you could chose to be intelligent or wise, which would you choose?

Have the participants share their answers with each other.

Read the **Plan and Purpose** article on page V-1. Ask the participants: "What does it mean to you that the Church teaches that Wisdom begins with "Fear of the Lord" and ends with "Love?"

Spiritual Awakening - Opening Prayer

Pray together the **Opening Prayer** at the top of insert page V-2.

Spiritual Awakening - Recognizing (5 minutes)

Ask for volunteers to read aloud each of the Scripture passages in the **Recognizing** section of **Spiritual Awakening** on insert page V-2. Remind the participants that each reader will pause for a few seconds of silence after each passage to allow anyone to offer any spontaneous thought, prayer, praise or thanksgiving that this Scripture might inspire.

Spiritual Awakening - Reflecting (20 minutes)

Read Chapter 9 of the Book of Wisdom (Page 687). Ask the participants: How significant was it for Solomon to ask for Wisdom when God would have given him any other gift (see 2 Chronicles 1:10). When do you think Wisdom is most appreciated in life? Like wisdom, what other God-given gifts are valued in today's culture?

Profile in Faith - (15 minutes)

Read the **Profile In Faith** article on Deborah on insert page V-3. Then, as a group, prayerfully read Chapter 5 of the Book of Judges, the "Canticle of Deborah" (Page 221). Discuss the answers to the following questions: How has God asked you to be a leader in your family, your parish, your community? Are you responding to His call? Share a time when you needed wisdom to handle a situation in your role as a wife, mother, daughter or leader in your parish or community.

Group Prayer (5 minutes)

Heavenly Father, open our eyes to Your wonder and our minds to Your infinite wisdom as we seek Your will in our lives. With a renewed awareness of the importance and meaning of Fear of the Lord, we offer these special prayers, praises and petitions: **enter aloud all individual intentions.** Give us the wisdom to make right choices always turning to You. In Jesus' name we pray, Amen.

Closing Prayer (10 minutes)

Leader: As a closing today, let us recite the Litany of the Holy Spirit.

Leader	Group
Lord have mercy on us.	Lord have mercy on us.
Christ have mercy on us.	Christ have mercy on us.
Lord have mercy on us.	Lord have mercy on us.
Father all powerful,	Have mercy on us.
Jesus, eternal Son of the Father, redeemer of the world,	Save us.
Spirit of the Father and the Son, boundless life of both,	Sanctify us.
Holy Trinity,	Hear Us!
Holy Spirit, who proceeds from the Father and the Son enter our hearts,	Enter our hearts.
Holy Spirit who art equal to the Father and the Son enter our hearts,	Enter our hearts.
Promise of God the Father,	Have mercy on us.
Ray of heavenly light,	Have mercy on us.
Author of all good,	Have mercy on us.
Source of heavenly water,	Have mercy on us.
Consuming fire,	Have mercy on us.
Ardent charity,	Have mercy on us.
Spiritual unction,	Have mercy on us.
Spirit of love and truth,	Have mercy on us.
Spirit of wisdom and understanding,	Have mercy on us.
Spirit of counsel and fortitude,	Have mercy on us.
Spirit of knowledge and piety,	Have mercy on us.
Spirit of the fear of the Lord,	Have mercy on us.
Spirit of grace and prayer,	Have mercy on us.
Spirit of peace and meekness,	Have mercy on us.
Spirit of modesty and innocence,	Have mercy on us.
Holy Spirit the comforter,	Have mercy on us.
Holy Spirit the sanctifier,	Have mercy on us.
Holy Spirit who governs the church,	Have mercy on us.
Gift of God the most high,	Have mercy on us.
Spirit who fills the universe,	Have mercy on us.
Spirit of the adoption of the children of God,	Have mercy on us.
Holy Spirit,	Inspire us with horror of sin.
Holy Spirit,	Come and renew the face of the earth.
Holy Spirit,	Shed the light in our souls.
Holy Spirit,	Engrave Thy Law in our hearts.
Holy Spirit,	Open to us the treasures of thy Graces.
Holy Spirit,	Teach us to pray well.

Holy Spirit,	Enlighten us with Thy heavenly inspirations.
Holy Spirit,	Lead us in the way of salvation.
Holy Spirit,	Grant us the only necessary knowledge.
Holy Spirit,	Inspire in us the practice of good.
Holy Spirit,	Grant us the merits of all virtues.
Holy Spirit,	Make us persevere in justice.
Holy Spirit,	Be thou our everlasting reward.
Lamb of God who takes away the sins of the world,	Send us Thy Holy Spirit.
Lamb of God who takes away the sins of the world,	Pour down into our soul the gifts of the Holy Spirit.
Lamb of God who takes away the sins of the world,	Grant us the Spirit of wisdom and piety.
Come, Holy Spirit! Fill the hearts of Thy faithful,	And enkindle in them the fire of Thy love.

Let Us Pray: Grant, O merciful Father, that Thy Divine Spirit may enlighten, inflame and purify us, that He may penetrate us with His heavenly dew and make us fruitful in good works, through Our Lord Jesus Christ, Thy Son, who with Thee, in the unity of the same Spirit, liveth and reigneth forever and ever. Amen.

Fellowship (15 minutes)

After the session is completed and while refreshments are served, play softly in the background: "Benediction" from the Faith-Filled Catholic Women's Bible Music CD.

The Faith-Filled Catholic Women's Bible Study Program

Participant's Worksheet

You can prepare for the discussion about the theme **Wisdom** by thinking about how you would answer the following questions:

My answers to the four quick questions:

1.

2.

3.

4.

Read the Plan and Purpose Article (Insert page V-1). "What does it mean to you that the Church teaches that Wisdom begins with "Fear of the Lord" and ends with Love?"

Read Chapter 9 of the Book of Wisdom (Page 687).

How significant was it for Solomon to ask for Wisdom when God would have given him any other gift?

When do I think Wisdom is most appreciated in life?

Like Wisdom, what other God-given gifts are valued in today's culture?

Read Chapter 5 of the Book of Judges, the "Canticle of Deborah" (Page 221).

How has God asked you to be a leader in your family, your parish, your community?

Share a time when you needed Wisdom to handle a situation in your role as a wife, mother, daughter, or leader in your parish or community.

Group Prayer - My intentions for group prayer this week:

Closing Prayer The Litany of the Holy Spirit

Lord have mercy on us.	Lord have mercy on us.
Christ have mercy on us.	Christ have mercy on us.
Lord have mercy on us.	Lord have mercy on us.
Father all powerful,	Have mercy on us.
Jesus, eternal Son of the Father, redeemer of the world,	Save us.
Spirit of the Father and the Son, boundless life of both,	Sanctify us.
Holy Trinity,	Hear Us.

Holy Spirit, who proceeds from
      the Father and the son enter our hearts,   Enter our hearts.
Holy Spirit Who art equal to the Father
      and the Son enter our hearts,   Enter our hearts.

Promise of God the Father,	Have mercy on us.
Ray of heavenly light,	Have mercy on us.
Author of all good,	Have mercy on us.
Source of heavenly water,	Have mercy on us.
Consuming fire,	Have mercy on us.
Ardent charity,	Have mercy on us.
Spiritual unction,	Have mercy on us.
Spirit of love and truth,	Have mercy on us.
Spirit of wisdom and understanding,	Have mercy on us.
Spirit of counsel and fortitude,	Have mercy on us.
Spirit of knowledge and piety,	Have mercy on us.
Spirit of the fear of the Lord,	Have mercy on us.
Spirit of grace and prayer,	Have mercy on us.
Spirit of peace and meekness,	Have mercy on us.
Spirit of modesty and innocence,	Have mercy on us.
Holy Spirit the comforter,	Have mercy on us.
Holy Spirit the sanctifier,	Have mercy on us.
Holy Spirit who governs the Church,	Have mercy on us.
Gift of God the most high,	Have mercy on us.
Spirit who fills the universe,	Have mercy on us.
Spirit of the adoption of the children of God,	Have mercy on us.
Holy Spirit,	Inspire us with horror of sin.
Holy Spirit,	Come and renew the face of the earth.
Holy Spirit,	Shed the light in our souls.
Holy Spirit,	Engrave Thy Law in our hearts.
Holy Spirit,	Open to us the treasures of they Graces.
Holy Spirit,	Teach us to pray well.
Holy Spirit,	Enlighten us with Thy heavenly inspirations.
Holy Spirit,	Lead us in the way of salvation.
Holy Spirit,	Grant us the only necessary knowledge.
Holy Spirit,	Inspire in us the practice of good.
Holy Spirit,	Grant us the merits of all virtues.
Holy Spirit,	Make us persevere in justice.
Holy Spirit,	Be thou our everlasting reward.
Lamb of God who takes away the sins of the world,	Send us Thy Holy Spirit.
Lamb of God who takes away the sins of the world,	Pour down into our soul the gifts of the Holy Spirit.
Lamb of God who takes away the sins of the world,	Grant us the Spirit of wisdom and piety.
Come, Holy Spirit! Fill the hearts of thy faithful,	And enkindle in them the fire of Thy love.

Let Us Pray: Grant, O merciful Father, that Thy Divine Spirit may enlighten, inflame and purify us, that He may penetrate us with His heavenly dew and make us fruitful in good works, through Our Lord Jesus Christ, Thy Son, who with Thee, in the unity of the same Spirit, lives and reigns forever and ever. Amen.

My Personal Response in Wisdom for this week - Teach the youth in your church by example and by gentle encouragement about the wisdom and appropriateness of proper dress and attire as a way to glorify God.

Other Scripture on **Wisdom**:

Mark 6:2 (Page 1072) * Luke 2:40 (Page 1096) * Luke 21:15 (Page 1128)

Acts 6:10 (Page 1177) * 1 Corinthians 1:21, 24, 30 (Page 1231)

Ephesians 1:8 (Page 1278) * Colossians 4:5 (Page 1297)

James 3:17 (Page 1344) * Revelation 17:9 (Page 1388)